LIFE WORLD LIBRARY

INDIA

LIFE WORLD LIBRARY

INDIA

by Joe David Brown

and The Editors of LIFE

TIME INCORPORATED · NEW YORK · 1961

COVER: Artfully
spreading powdered pigments,
Indian girls decorate an airfield
apron as a welcome greeting
for an arriving dignitary.

ABOUT THE WRITER

Joe David Brown, who wrote the interpretive text for this volume of the
LIFE World Library, gained his understanding of India during the years
he spent as a wide-ranging correspondent for the New Delhi Bureau of
TIME and LIFE Magazines. A journalist with many years experience on
various newspapers throughout the country, Mr. Brown joined the staff
of Time Inc. in 1952. An Alabaman by birth, he served as National Affairs writer for TIME and later as a TIME-LIFE correspondent in England,
France and India. Since 1958 he has been a freelance writer and has published two successful novels, *Stars In My Crown* and *Kings Go Forth*.

Contents

TIME INC. BOOK DIVISION

Editor
NORMAN P. ROSS

Copy Director   *Art Director*
WILLIAM JAY GOLD   EDWARD A. HAMILTON

Chief of Research
BEATRICE T. DOBIE

Editorial staff for "India":

Editor, LIFE World Library	OLIVER E. ALLEN
Assistant to the Editor	JAY BRENNAN
Designer	BEN SCHULTZ
Chief Researcher	GRACE BRYNOLSON
Researchers	RUTH GALAID, JEAN SULZBERGER, IRENE ERTUGRUL, NANCY JONES, HELEN R. TURVEY, BARBARA BALLANTINE, SHEILA OSMUNDSEN, KIP SERRA, LINDA WOLFE
Picture Researchers	MARGARET K. GOLDSMITH, JOAN T. LYNCH
Art Associates	ALBERT J. DUNN, ROBERT L. YOUNG
Art Assistants	JAMES D. SMITH, RICHARD FORTE, JOHN M. WOODS
Copy Staff	MARIAN GORDON GOLDMAN, ANN SHAW, DOLORES A. LITTLES

•

Publisher	JEROME S. HARDY
General Manager	JOHN A. WATTERS

•

LIFE MAGAZINE

Editor   *Managing Editor*   *Publisher*
EDWARD K. THOMPSON   GEORGE P. HUNT   C. D. JACKSON

•

The text for the chapters of this book was written by Joe David Brown and for the picture essays by Walter Karp and Thomas Wheeler. The following individuals and departments of LIFE Magazine helped in producing the book: James Burke, Margaret Bourke-White, Eliot Elisofon, Dmitri Kessel, Leonard McCombe, Howard Sochurek and Hank Walker, staff photographers; Charles Mohr and James Shepherd of the New Delhi Bureau; Gene Farmer, Foreign News Editor; and Doris O'Neil, Chief of the LIFE Picture Library. Valuable assistance was also given by Donald Bermingham, Time Inc. Foreign News Service; Content Peckham, Chief of the Time Inc. Bureau of Editorial Reference; and Don Connery, former Chief of the New Delhi Bureau.

Introduction

As the author states at the outset of this volume, it is not easy for Westerners to understand India. This is perhaps especially true of Americans, for during the days when the British ruled India the United States had little contact with the subcontinent. And it was only natural that when India faced west it should look to Britain, with whom it had such close political, commercial and social ties.

But with independence the new India opened its windows to the world. Freedom was only the beginning. In his moving speech on the eve of independence, Mr. Nehru warned that the future "is not one of ease or resting but of incessant striving. . . ."

How the Indian government and people have embarked on this great adventure—something of their problems, the immense difficulties encountered, their frustrations and failures, but also their achievements and victories—will be found here in the text by Joe David Brown and in the fascinating picture essays.

As India bent to these formidable tasks, it found a sympathetic reaction in the United States. The American people had always supported India's aspirations for independence and they now set out to discover this land which for so long had been a mystery.

But more than curiosity was involved. There was a growing awareness that this vast land of India, with more than 400 million people, was a great testing ground which might determine whether people's wants and expectations could be met by democratic processes. The direction it took could well determine the direction in which other newly independent countries of Asia and Africa would go.

That India is developing an economic and social system adapted to its own needs and genius is, I think, apparent. The process is one involving trial and error, and flexibility. The system is fundamentally democratic and so seeks not only social justice but the improvement of the quality of its citizens, for on this all progress ultimately depends.

That there were and still are many obstacles to overcome is undeniable. Yet these problems were faced with courage and vision, and if one reviews the achievements of the intervening years one must count them impressive. Improvement in living standards has kept ahead of population growth, and progress has been made in education, health and the social services. In 1960 India's rate of industrial growth was among the world's highest. The country has adopted a fiscal austerity which might well serve as a model for many countries with far longer experience in self-government. The roots of democracy are striking deeper.

These achievements compel our admiration. But if we are to understand India's purposes and ideals we shall need to know more than facts. We shall need to learn as well something about the country's religion, its philosophy, and the customs, traditions and habits of thought of its people. Yet the effort cannot help but be enormously worthwhile. We shall be rewarded by experiencing the friendship of the Indian people. We shall be stimulated by their intelligence, captivated by their charm and dignity, and touched by their kindliness and tolerance. And we shall learn that Indians profoundly believe that freedom and dignity need not be sacrificed to progress.

ELLSWORTH BUNKER
former U.S. Ambassador to India

1

A Society Distinctive and Enigmatic

IT is not easy for a Westerner—or even for many Easterners—to comprehend, much less appreciate, the sprawling, elusive, exasperating, preposterous and wondrous country that is India. Few lands hold such a power to shock— and to enthrall. Today India is better known in the West than it has ever been in the past; its statesmen speak a language fully comprehensible to their hearers in the council chambers of the world. There is communication on a technical level, too. Indian workmen may be clad in unfamiliar garments, yet the processes by which the country's steel ingots are produced and the waters of its mighty rivers are

dammed are easily understood in Pittsburgh and the Tennessee Valley, and the atmosphere of an India that is modernizing itself is metaphorically as electric as the products of its big new dams. Urged on by English-speaking Indian politicians, India's engineers prod the land and their countrymen into the 20th Century with the aid of western blueprints. But the outward appearance of communication is deceptive. The true meeting of eastern and western thought processes has not yet taken place. Merely beginning to unravel the dense fabric that is Indian thought involves an investigation into a society more distinctively different from western civilization than any other on earth.

Consider the strange and fascinating deity called Shiva. As one of Hinduism's great triad, Shiva is a profound influence on untold millions of devout Indians. The worship of Shiva is probably the oldest living faith of mankind, having been practiced in the Indus Valley for around 5,000 years. In Hinduism's firmament, Brahma is the lord of all creation and Vishnu the lord of preservation; Shiva, the third member of the triumvirate, is the god of destruction and re-creation. As such he possesses a multitude of physical, moral and spiritual attributes, some of them outwardly contradictory. For example, even though Shiva is the destroyer, he is associated with the lingam, primitive symbol of fertility. Pious Hindus hold that destruction is only the necessary prelude to creation in this universe of endless cycles of repetition, where all things are in a constant and endless process of being destroyed and being reborn.

Shiva has a thousand names, among them the Great Lord (because in him is All) and Shishu (which means the crescent moon, a promise of life). Some of the time he is depicted in his home on Mount Kailas, a sacred peak in the Himalayas, where he lives in a celestial palace and is worshiped by other gods and *rishis,* or seers; at other times he is shown as a mendicant, wearing ragged robes and carrying a begging bowl in his hand. Sometimes he frequents cremation grounds where he is the lord of ghosts; at other times he withdraws from the world and goes to Kailas, where he sits under a tree and practices the most fearsome austerities, because he is also the Mahayogi, the great ascetic.

But one of Shiva's most popular images is as Nataraja, Lord of the Dance. For Shiva is the god of rhythm and in Hindu mysticism he

SHIVA'S DANCE, fiery and graceful, shows him as lord of cosmic rhythm and energy, one of his many roles.

embodies cosmic energy; his dance represents the "activity" of God, and this activity is understood to occur within men. As is written in one of the many Hindu scriptural manuals: "The dancing foot, the sound of tinkling bells /The songs that are sung and the varying steps /The form assumed by our Dancing Gurupara /Find out these within yourself, then shall your fetters fall away."

An ordinary Westerner, even though he may cherish or tolerate doctrinal myths in his own religion, is almost certain to find the concept of Shiva fanciful in the extreme. For he does not know that there is more to it than meets the western eye. Shiva is the destroyer—but the object of his destructive efforts is the prison that binds each separate soul. The Westerner may be revolted when he visits Benares, Shiva's holy city, and sees bodies being cremated beside the Ganges River—but cremation is believed by Hindus to burn away the illusions that prevent men from seeing the truth about themselves. Learned Indians explain that many-sided Shiva, with all the seeming contradictions in his personality, is the god who most nearly symbolizes the Hindu spirit, and that Shiva's story is a true reading of the emotional and contemplative palimpsest which represents Hindu thought and character.

The degree of rapport a Westerner feels toward such thinking will very largely determine his capacity for understanding India. For there are two great facts of India, perhaps the only facts that are wholly true about a country that has such a lavish variety of languages, customs and beliefs. One of these facts is Hinduism. The other is poverty. The visitor must try to grasp the complexities of one and look beyond the ugliness of the other before he can truly know the country. Only then will he be likely to comprehend the country's special character, which proceeds from its philosophy and is based first and foremost on a centuries-old effort to understand the meaning and ultimate purpose of life.

THE history of India is closely linked to the history of Hinduism, and the two are so entwined that it is impossible to examine one without taking into account the other. Elements of Hinduism can be traced back to the dawn of Indian civilization around 4000 B.C. The faith was a force in India when Moses descended Mount Sinai with the Ten Commandments; it was already firmly guiding every phase of Indian life long before western man groped his way from the murk of the Dark Ages. Modern India is officially a secular state but its progressive programs must be carried out in the face of the fact that 85 per cent of India's 438 million people are Hindus. Moreover, many of them are rigidly orthodox in their belief, and to the extent that they are able to do so they cling fast to all of Hinduism's manifold customs and prejudices. The government has mounted a steady campaign to rout out certain customs embedded in Hinduism, such as untouchability and child marriage, and in the cities these practices have been considerably reduced. But in the villages, where most of the country's population is found, the patterns of a thousand years are not changed easily. A century ago the British outlawed *suttee*, or self-cremation, but a devout Hindu widow occasionally still throws herself into the flames of her husband's funeral pyre.

Hinduism is generally described as a religion but it is far more than that, and in the western sense that religion is thought to be confined to creed and worship, the description is misleading. Hinduism is a complete rule of life, and every act of the orthodox Hindu's existence — rising in the morning, bathing, eating, praying, even the sex act — is regulated by rituals.

But the rules of Hinduism may be interpreted one way in one community and quite a different way in another. The country's modern leader, Prime Minister Jawaharlal Nehru, once observed that India contains all that is disgusting and all that is noble. The same can be said of Hinduism. At its highest level it is a lofty speculative philosophy, mystic and monotheistic, which enjoins an ascetic rejection of the world of the flesh because it considers man's earthly span as only a passing moment in the soul's long journey through time. At its worst it is a museum of primitive superstition which separates men at birth and for the rest of their lives limits their ambitions and opportunities by its institutions of caste.

Hinduism's great strength is that it rejects nothing. As a result it has never been supplanted in India by other religions, but has instead absorbed them. It is, of course, the basis for India's time-honored reputation for spirituality and mysticism. There are some genuine riddles hidden within the occult realms of Hinduism and they baffle reputable scientists as much as they awe uneducated peasants.

FOR better or worse, Hinduism has endowed India with a character and outlook that is unique, for the country's customs and beliefs are ingrained in a tradition which recognizes the unity of all life in a way that is not shared by the rest of mankind. Hinduism also has shaped a mind which is unlike any other in the world. This mind is not, however, one to which Westerners can readily adjust.

At its noblest the Hindu mind is philosophical, richly cultural and capable of a serene detachment that not only impresses but in a mysterious manner seems to shed a peaceful radiance on those who come under its influence. Many Indian religious leaders and mystics have possessed this gift, and for some Westerners Gandhi, the political leader, also had it. Countless hard-bitten journalists who came to scoff or probe curiously at this unprepossessing gap-toothed man in a loincloth went away to write glowingly of his beneficent presence. But the same traditions which can make a superior mind philosophical may make an ordinary one merely contentious. Instead of being cultural the mind may be narrowly parochial, and instead of detached and serene it may be indifferent and smug.

While the Hindu mind can be baffling to a visitor, India's scalding poverty almost always comes as a shock. The visitor may have heard that India's per capita income is only $70 a year or less than two cents a day, that the Indian's life expectancy—despite recent efforts which have lengthened it—is still only 42 years, and that 76 per cent of the population is illiterate. But he seldom fully grasps the meaning of these dismal statistics until he sees them translated into human terms: the thousands of homeless, ragged figures sleeping in the streets and alleys of Bombay and other cities.

Several countries in Asia are almost as poor as India, but India's poverty generally seems more overwhelming. One obvious reason is that in comparison with what appears to be the conspicuous light-heartedness of other Asians like the Burmese or the Malays, the Indians seem to be a solemn people. There is relatively little laughter or other overt sign of gaiety as they swarm endlessly through the streets of the large cities, or gather to bathe in the scum-covered tanks in the villages, or even when they hunker down in small groups to share a bubble pipe in the shade of a banyan tree. Another reason is that the vast majority of Indians seldom complain about their underprivileged condition. Some observers claim that this is a heritage of Hinduism. When an Indian's crops fail or his water buffalo dies, he is likely to blame it on sins he committed in a previous existence.

THE shocked Westerner, conditioned as he is to believe that life is of supreme value and that human misery should not go unattended, is often frustrated and affronted when he encounters such large-scale suffering. Especially if he is not prepared to make the great efforts required of serious understanding, he is offended by the endless, faceless crowds and by his periodic brushes with disease. Here are millions of unlettered, hungry human beings who seem to cry out for help, but there is nothing he can do about it. Once this process starts, the Westerner can find much to dislike about India.

If he does reach this stage, moreover, the Westerner never truly gets to know India or Indians. He treats the country as a vast slum and he passes through it as quickly as possible on his way to hotels, clubs or air-conditioned bungalows in well-kept foreign enclaves. Such an isolation usually brings on a peculiar affliction known in British times as sahib-sickness ("sahib" is a word for gentleman or master). Besides making its victim testy and giving him delusions of grandeur to varying degrees, this affliction makes the Westerner blind to all that is worthwhile and exciting in the ancient land in which he lives.

THE outsider who does not blind himself, however, will be richly rewarded. To many, there is an air of timelessness and continuity in this great domain whose people, united by a single powerful philosophy, have lived through so many centuries of conquerors and overlords and managed through it all to preserve unique traditions of beauty and order. There is a subtlety and sophistication of outlook—a willingness to see matters in shades of gray rather than in black and white—that is born of countless epochs of witnessing and suffering.

There is a feeling of hospitality and generosity, particularly in rural byways, that can prove almost embarrassing to the visitor whose car has broken down and who finds himself besieged by scores of friendly, chattering villagers offering all manner of suggestions of help. There also is a sense of personal discipline, a nobility and grace of the individual, which can be epitomized in the rhythmic, stately walk of women bearing pots of water on their heads from the village well. There is often a certain dignity amid the poverty, an ability to ignore the squalor which time has brought and to rise above it.

Illiteracy and superstition may be rife, but few people have a higher regard for knowledge and wisdom than do the Indians. The creator

Brahma is also the teacher, and in a land where men are honored and revered for abandoning material pursuits and taking to the contemplative life, it is no accident of politics that Prime Minister Nehru happens to be one of the world's most noted thinkers and writers. Nowhere else can there be found such a remarkable respect for all organic life—a veneration which extends to the most minute of the earth's creatures.

Finally, India today has an excitement about it, a vibrant air caused by its abrupt arrival in the modern age. In this land of extremes that seems to have a superfluity of everything— more beauty, more poverty, more gods and goddesses, more beggars—the vast potential represented by the country's new industrial development is one that can only provoke awe. Here is a colossus awakening and beginning to flex its muscles, and no one can say what it may do or where it may be headed.

Getting to know India is especially difficult because the country is so big. It is the seventh largest country in size, about the size of all Europe outside Russia, but it is the second largest in the world in population (the first being Red China). No part of the world is better marked off by nature as a region than the Indian subcontinent. Bounded by the Himalayas on the north, it stretches southward for some 2,000 miles before it tapers off into the Indian Ocean, with the Bay of Bengal on the east and the Arabian Sea on the west. No one looking at a map would ever guess that such a well-defined country could contain such a fantastic conglomeration of peoples, languages, customs, colors, animals and weather.

INDIA seems more like a dozen countries than one, and for most of its long history it was. With the exception of certain great imperial periods scattered throughout its history, the area now called India was for centuries a patchwork of heterogeneous nation-states that were constantly arranged and rearranged as one conqueror defeated another. As recently as 1947, when India won its independence from Britain, the country was still splintered into British India and 562 princely states. Some of these units were nothing more than small estates, but others were as large as European countries and had their own armies, currencies and postal systems. A traveler driving 30 miles through western India's Kathiawar peninsula, an area studded with 450 petty states, would be stopped at least 15 times for customs inquiries.

India is so vast and diversified that it makes a mockery of any generalization. Take the weather. India is known as a cruelly hot country, and for most of the hot season, which extends through April and May, as well as for much of the rainy season, which is brought on by the annual downpour of the summer monsoon and lasts from June through September, much of India does suffer acutely from heat or humidity or both. Midday temperatures may range from well over 100 degrees in the shade in New Delhi to 120 degrees at some outpost in the Thar Desert of northwest India.

Yet at most of the hill stations perched on foothills of the Himalayas in north India the climate is pleasant and even bracing all the year round. The cold-weather season, which begins with December and ends with March, is a comfortable time throughout most of India, and in the north—in New Delhi, for example—a light coat is needed in the evenings. The climate in Kashmir is somewhat like that of Switzerland, and of course the farther one ventures into the lofty Himalayan area, the majestic Abode of Snow which fringes a good part of India's northern frontier, the colder the weather gets. At least 40 peaks in this awe-inspiring chain exceed 25,000 feet. Yet 2,000 miles to the south, the entire tip of India is a luxuriant tropical land studded with palm trees and beaches of golden sand and inhabited by people who live in huts made of palm fronds.

CONTRASTS are commonplace. The broad Punjab, which lies just below the foothills of the Himalayas, is a rich land which produces India's highest wheat yield, but directly southwest of it are the shimmering deserts of Rajasthan, where there is not enough water to support life. Cherrapunji, a village in Assam, is one of the wettest spots on earth, with an average annual rainfall of 451.6 inches. Raindrops as large as marbles fall on Cherrapunji during the monsoon season, and the wind sometimes drives them with such velocity that the inhabitants of the town dress in armor made of wicker and carry small wicker shields to protect themselves. Farther westward, the Indo-Gangetic Plain is formed by the basins of three distinct river systems (the Indus, the Ganges and the Brahmaputra), and almost every year floods sweep away whole villages and drown hundreds of people.

The great Indo-Gangetic Plain is also one of nature's wonders: 1,900 miles long and 90 to 200 miles wide, it is the greatest stretch of alluvial plain in the world and also one of the most densely populated. For nearly 1,000 miles of its length, this fabled flatland drops less than 700 feet in elevation.

Some 40,000 Indians—almost one every 15 minutes—are killed each year by poisonous snakes and wild animals. Herds of wild monkeys frequently pillage villages in the south, and when packs of wolves and hyenas were driven out of their lairs several years ago by a jungle clearance project in Uttar Pradesh state, they invaded the busy capital city of Lucknow and carried off more than 30 children. The terror was ended only after army troops threw a cordon around the city.

TIGERS are a menace in some parts of India, and once a lone rhinoceros killed three men and kept the entire population of a sizeable town in northern Assam barricaded behind locked doors for days before it wandered away. Packs of jackals occasionally rove even the most elegant residential sections of New Delhi at night; their eerie howls sometimes awaken guests in hotels which are as palatial and luxurious as any in the world.

India has no common language, and the vast majority of Indians are unable to communicate with one another once they leave their home districts (in some rare cases even after they leave their own villages). Altogether some 845 languages and dialects are spoken within the borders of India, although most of these are relatively unimportant in terms of numbers of speakers, and the Indian constitution gives official status to only 14 of them. English is scheduled to lose its position soon as an official medium of communication, but most educated Indians speak it, the top government officials use it and most of the proceedings in Parliament and in the Supreme Court are in English.

This odd situation has arisen because in the hot flush of nationalism which followed independence, India decided to replace English with a national language of its own and chose

Hindi, a Sanskrit-derived tongue of north central India written in Devanagari script. The constitution provides that Hindi will replace English in 1965, but there seems to be little chance that this deadline can be met. A great many top Indian officials still do not speak it, and strong pressure is being brought by non-Hindu regions (especially Bengal and southern India) to extend the deadline. Hindi or its closely related variants, Hindustani and Urdu, is used by roughly 40 per cent of the country, but it is a north India language and completely foreign in the south where the chief languages have a different base.

The abandoning of English is a particularly sore point with many of the country's educators, who say that translating technical works and the best of world literature into Hindi is a task almost too gigantic to consider. It is largely because of their efforts that English continues to be a required subject in the upper grades of some public schools and has for the present been retained as the language of instruction in most universities, although this has caused persistent controversy. An Indian who is not so fortunate as to be born in a Hindi-speaking northern state has to learn at least three languages if he aspires to advancement in the civil service. He must retain his mother tongue for personal use, know enough Hindi to pass his examinations and learn English as well, for English is an indispensable requirement for any top level government post.

Language is a great barrier and a great problem in India. Daily news bulletins of the All-India Radio are broadcast in Hindi, English, Bengali, Oriya, Tamil, Telugu, Kanarese, Malayalam, Punjabi, Marathi, Gujarati, Assamese,

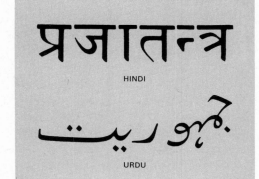

HINDI

URDU

LANGUAGE BARRIERS are exemplified by the contrast between Hindi, recently chosen as India's national tongue—but unknown to millions—and Urdu, the language of educated Moslems and innumerable others. The words above mean democracy. Hindi and Urdu are both varieties of Hindustani; Urdu, written from right to left, has Persian influences; Hindi, written from left to right, is based on Sanskrit.

Urdu, Kashmiri and Konkani—and there still are large numbers of Indians (like the aboriginal hill tribesmen) who would not understand any of these.

Racially speaking, there is no such thing as an Indian. The original inhabitants of the subcontinent are believed to have been a Negroid people ethnically related to the aborigines of Ceylon, Sumatra and possibly even Australia. At some prehistoric stage it is thought that a migration of what are loosely called Dravidian races began to infiltrate India. The Dravidians probably came from western Asia and it seems likely that they traveled by way of Baluchistan. Over the centuries, successive waves of migrants and conquerors followed the Dravidians, and today six basic racial strains and nine sub-groupings can be traced in India, though most ethnologists agree that these classifications are often used without relation to linguistic or historical fact and are mere labels.

Broadly speaking, the fair or partially fair strains in India are found in the mountain valleys in the northwest, where they are mixed with Mediterranean and Oriental strains. They can be easily distinguished from the Mediterranean strains found mostly on the plains. Older and darker peoples are found everywhere, but Mongoloid elements, often mixed with other strains, are common in the hill regions in the north and east.

Within India's borders are found all the skin tones known to man. There are millions of black-skinned tribal people in India, and there are young business executives in Bombay who look as if they had just arrived from Damascus. Many of India's hill people are indistinguishable from Tibetans, and in Calcutta's bazaars are merchants who would look at home in the markets of Istanbul. In general, the people of south India are darker than those from the north, but there are many exceptions. There are Indians who live in tents and in caves and some who boast modernistic apartment dwellings designed by the contemporary architect Le Corbusier. India has mountain gypsies and nomad tribes wandering the plains and maharajas who live in palaces that already were old when the United States became a nation.

Indians themselves often are astounded to discover how many racial strains and levels of civilization exist in their country. They flock in droves to the Republic Day dance festival held in New Delhi each year, gawking at the scores of Indian tribes that put on exhibitions of dancing, stilt-walking and acrobatics. Many of the tribal groups are virtually unknown outside their own regions, and it was only by seeing them at the festival that most Indians learned that there was a people in Assam which was descended from a vanished civilization east of the Himalayas, or a pure African tribe in Hyderabad which was descended from slaves imported two centuries ago and which had managed to preserve its identity and culture.

ONE significant group not represented at the festival consists of the four million-odd members of the so-called Criminal tribes. These bands live mostly in the north, and their ancestral occupations were robbery, swindling and vice. The British long ago decided that the Criminal tribes were hereditary evildoers and that nothing much could be done about them, except to keep them under as much surveillance as possible. It was taken for granted that a member of one of these tribes was a criminal from the time of his birth. One of the early reforms instigated by independent India was a program to rehabilitate the Criminal tribes. The criminal label was removed and self-help programs were instituted. While a few tribes today still are said to follow their hereditary professions as prostitutes, pickpockets, thieves and swindlers, many have turned to lawful pursuits.

Is prolific old India with its seemingly infinite diversity of blood, color, language, dress, manners and social cleavages truly a nation? Can democratic institutions stand the stresses and strains imposed by the interplay of such diverse forces? These are touchy questions in India, and they are resented by the many Indians who are fiercely proud of their country's progress since independence was won in 1947. They point out, and most scholars agree with them, that India has always had a deep underlying unity, based on a common culture which is receptive and adaptable. They claim that political cohesion is a comparatively recent phenomenon only because a lack of transportation and communication and a progression of conquerors and overlords kept India divided and subdivided for centuries.

Nevertheless a decade and a half is only a passing moment in the history of a country at least 5,000 years old. No matter how sympathetic or partisan one is toward the new and independent India, it still is too soon to accept the unity of the subcontinent as an established fact. There was nothing predestined and automatic about the creation of that unity: the making of modern India was seared by chaos and bloodshed in the 1940s when two great chunks of territory were torn away to form the new and independent state of Pakistan. Today there seems little doubt that many Kashmiris and many Naga tribesmen along the Assam border, if given a free choice, would vote for greater autonomy or even for secession from India. Agitation for separate states on the basis of language also plagues India and keeps it from being a completely united nation with a cohesive society.

INDIA is faced with many formidable and terrifying problems. As it fights to solve them and to go forward, it must at the same time struggle against innumerable social, religious and cultural anachronisms which tend to keep it tied to the past. Since 1947 much progress has been made, but the battle for a modern, unified India is only just beginning.

Placid cows park on a busy sidewalk in a Punjabi town. Sacred to Hindus, India's cows are free to wander at will on city streets.

Capacious Home for the Unexpected

In the turbulent mass of Indian civilization, every variety of human and animal life has a lodging place. Cave-dwelling hermits are revered and haggling tradesmen are respected. Sacred cows roam busy streets where holy men jostle westernized bureaucrats. A Communist harangues a crowd and nearby a Hindu teacher discourses on the scriptures. Digesting everything, rejecting nothing, India accumulates incongruities, dazzling visitors from tidier lands.

17

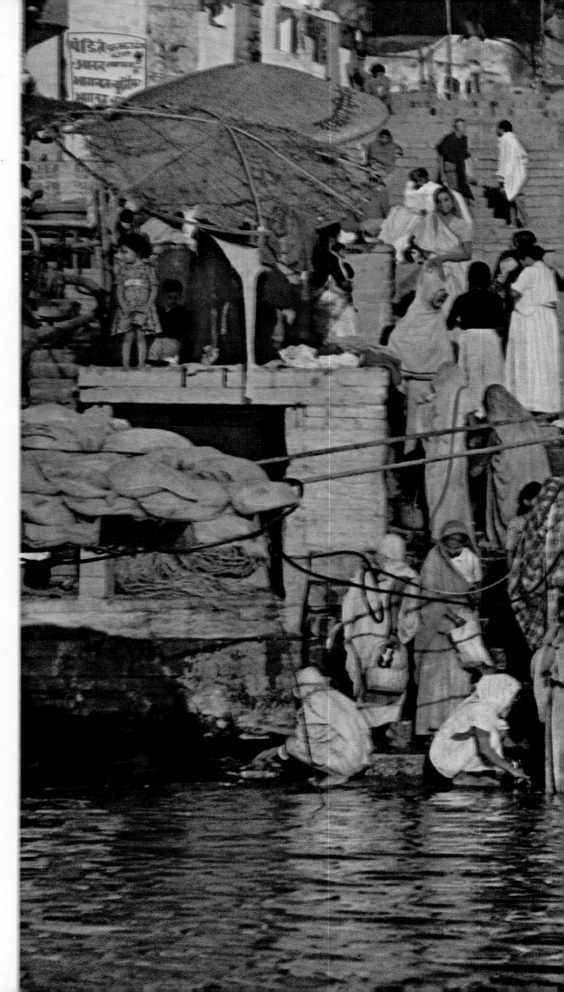

RELIGIOUS RITE, bathing in the sacred Ganges River is practiced by Hindu women at a stone landing in the holy city of Benares. Hindus, who must bathe before their daily prayers, have set up these landings, known as *ghats*, all along the rivers.

SARI-CLAD WOMAN sifts a heap of fiery dye (*above*), which is used to emblazon India's renowned silk and cotton fabrics.

MODERN THOROUGHFARE in Bombay (*below*) swarms with strollers. Their turbans when unwound may measure 18 feet.

VIBRANT MOSAIC, the vivid landscape is startlingly crowded with people

प्रहमडावाद - महमाना

AGILE TRAVELERS escape the blistering heat of an Indian train by clambering out on the window ledges as it stops on a siding. Heat, dust, erratic service and skillful thieves often plague the passengers on India's colonial-vintage trains, but the British-built Indian railway system is, nonetheless, the most extensive network in Asia.

DEFT GESTURES punctuate the performance of a ritual dance dedicated to the god Krishna. The swaying dancers, wearing skirts flecked with tiny mirrors, employ scores of formalized movements, each of which has a precise symbolic meaning.

IN A MARKET, muscular women use metal pails to wash off urns. Although most Indian women work hard and enjoy few freedoms or luxuries, women of means can be strikingly decorative. Typically adorned, the woman opposite rims her eyes with black pigment, wears a beauty mark on her forehead and a jewel nose ornament.

WOMEN, *rooted in their families, remain the graceful subordinates of men*

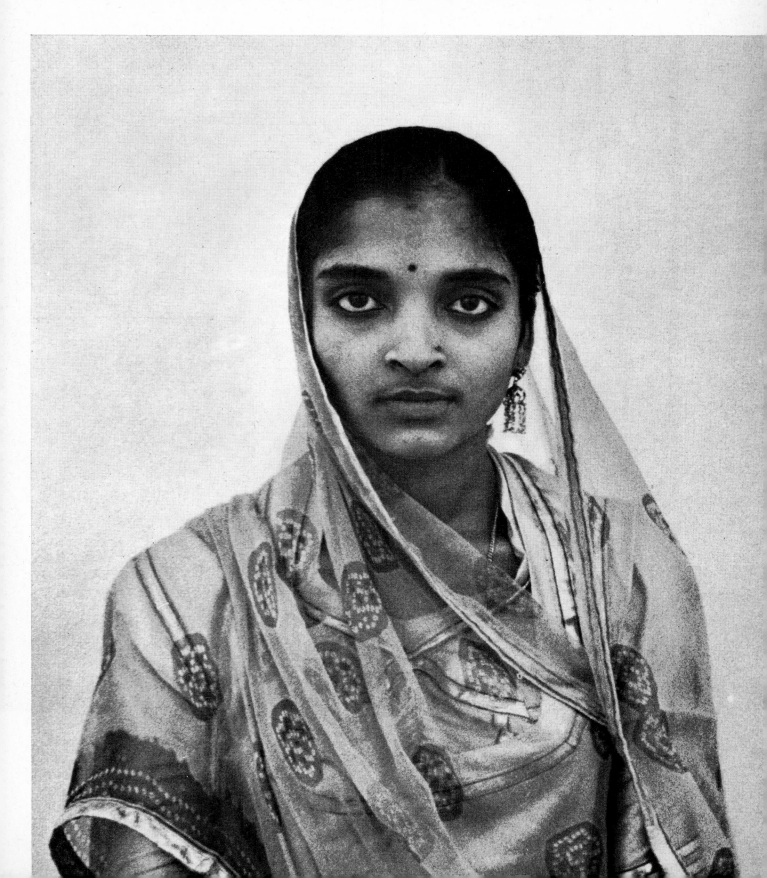

BRICK-DRY TOWN, baking under a pitiless sky, may get no rain for the eight months preceding the monsoon season.

MUDDY FIELDS glisten with patches of flood brought by monsoon rains. The rain's timely onslaught saves the crops.

27

HOLY MEN, Hinduism's extreme ascetics smear themselves with ashes as part of a purification ritual. Thousands of holy men wander homeless through India.

2

A Preoccupation with the Spirit

WHEN Alexander the Great, having conquered most of mankind, was resting with his armies on the Indus Plain in the pleasant spring of 326 B.C., he turned his attention one day to a group of Indian holy men sitting naked in the sun, oblivious to the world around them. Curious, the great conqueror dispatched Onesicritus, one of his brightest young officers, to find out what manner of men they were and what wisdom they had to impart. The holy men told Onesicritus that to try to pass on their knowledge to his master through interpreters would be like trying to make water flow clear through many layers of mud. If the mighty Alexander wished to acquire their wisdom, they continued, let him begin by stripping off his fine robes and coming to sit humbly with them in the sun.

From the earliest of contacts, western man has never ceased to marvel at the overwhelming religiosity of Holy India. India indeed has encompassed almost every shade and kind of religious belief and practice the world has ever known. In the jungles of south and central India live aborigines who still practice the primitive animism which is believed to be the earliest of man's religions and which maintains that every object in the universe is inhabited by an individual spirit. Most of the subcontinent's Mohammedans now live in Pakistan, but there are still some 35.4 million Moslems in India itself. Buddhism, which originated in India in the Sixth Century B.C. as a sort of Protestant Reformation against the Hinduism of its day, has largely taken root elsewhere. It claims only 200,000 followers in its native land. Jainism, an ascetic heresy which originated in the same period as Buddhism, maintains an influence out of proportion to the number (about 1.6 million) of its believers. By tradition, Christianity was brought to India by that doubting apostle, St. Thomas; there are now about 8.2 million Christians in the country. There are also some 6.2 million Sikhs, who maintain a fierce dislike of Moslems, although their religion contains elements of Mohammedanism as well as Hinduism, and about 100,000 Zoroastrians, or Parsis, who are mainly bankers and merchants.

THE overwhelmingly dominant religion of India is the faith which the West calls Hinduism and its own 300 million followers call *Dharma*—variously translated as Harmony, Order, and Law. Hinduism is the all-pervasive fact of Indian life, and its teachings far transcend traditional religious areas. It is simultaneously a theology, a philosophy, a social system and a way of life. The scriptures of Hinduism are so abundant and complex that young Hindus have traditionally had little time to study anything else. Its gods are equally abundant. Though the popular figure of 330 million is not the result of an actual count but intended to suggest infinity, the Hindu pantheon in fact contains literally hundreds of different deities and semideities. Images of them, often many-limbed and animal-faced, abound in temples and roadside nooks. A popular god such as Shiva may appear in a thousand guises. Almost every act and waking hour of the pious Hindu involves a ritual of some sort, to a degree which has made some western observers call India a "nation of priests." The West's nearest approach to a society like India's was medieval Christendom, when all life revolved around the common faith and the Church stoutly supported the socioeconomic system of feudalism that so strongly resembles Hinduism's caste system.

Hinduism has not, of course, been the sole influence in Indian history. On the contrary, many observers believe that India's centuries of poverty, invasions, war, flood and famine may be responsible for the national tendency to despair of this world and seek happiness elsewhere. But Hinduism has unquestionably been the major influence in the shaping of Indian thought. As such, it may rightly claim major responsibility for both India's glory and its misery. It has advanced its people's spiritual growth while retarding their material progress. Its multiplicity of castes and sects has been and remains profoundly divisive. Yet it is doubtful that India—divided also by language and race and tradition and, until very recent times, by political separation into 562 principalities—could have emerged as a nation without the unifying bond of a common religion.

The question of whether Hinduism is in fact a common religion comes naturally to Westerners confronted by Hinduism's extraordinary variety of beliefs, practices and gods, its tolerant conviction that all religions are essentially the same and its eclectic tendency to absorb the ideas, beliefs and spiritual heroes of other and far different faiths.

HEARING Hinduism fiercely condemned—often by Hindus themselves—as a superstitious and backward escapism, and hearing it as ardently championed by both eastern and western intellectuals, Westerners may understandably have less trouble in making up their minds about Hinduism than in simply understanding it. One American scholar has asserted flatly that "Hinduism is the most confused, confusing and distinctive of all the world's religions." It has no founder, no central authority or organization, no fixed creed.

If Hinduism seems less a single religion than a sort of theological grab bag of beliefs and practices from which the individual can select whatever suits him, the impression is in large measure correct. Often considered mystically impractical, Hinduism is supremely realistic in its recognition that people are different—not only individually but at different stages of their lives—and that they therefore need different ways of approaching God. In the millenniums of its existence, Hinduism has devised ways for all manner of men, at all ages and at all levels. It offers that which its followers believe is best suited to a man's station in life. The illiterate peasant, finding most of the color and drama of his life in ceremonies, processions and festivals celebrating his favorite religious myths, may seem—or actually may be—idolatrous of his household and village gods. The intellectual Hindu, on the other hand, is a firm believer in monotheism. To him, Hinduism's hundreds of dissimilar god-images are but symbols of the countless aspects and infinite power of the single God or Supreme Reality, which—or whom—he calls Brahman or Brahma. He is confident that in God's own good time, in this life or in some future incarnation, every human being will eventually put away childish things and know the boundless and eternal joy of union with Truth. A conviction of man's ultimate nature and destiny provides the basic unity within Hinduism's bewildering diversity.

THE origins of Hinduism are lost in prehistory. Certainly it is a very old religion. Elements of it were brought to India as a form of primitive nature worship by the Aryan invaders who began surging in from the northwest about the middle of the second millennium B.C. (See Chapter 3.) Its earliest expression is in the four collections of sacred hymns and prayers and ancient magic runes and spells called the Vedas. Hindus believe that the Vedas, transmitted orally from generation to generation, have existed always; western scholars concede that some of their contents are at least 4,000 years old.

The most famous and poetic of the four, the Rig-Veda, reached final form in the Eighth Century B.C. Its *mantras* (stanzas of praise) are addressed mainly to such nature deities as Indra, god of storms and war; Agni, god of fire; and Soma, god of the intoxicating juice which the Aryans squeezed from the soma plant.

> *We have drunk Soma and become*
> *immortal;*
> *We have attained the light, the gods*
> *discovered.*
> *What can hostility now do against us?*
> *And what, immortal god, the spite of*
> *mortals?*

The Rig-Veda contains intimations, however, that something more than flights of intoxication is required to explain the universe and shape men's destiny. Varuna, originally god of the sky, has become the keeper of universal order, moral as well as physical.

> *If we have sinned against the man who*
> *loves us, have ever wronged a brother,*
> *friend or comrade,*
> *The neighbor ever with us, or a stranger,*
> *O Varuna, remove from us the*
> *trespass.*
> *If we, as gamesters, cheat at play, have*
> *cheated, done wrong unwittingly or*
> *sinned of purpose,*
> *Cast all these sins away like loosened*
> *fetters, and, Varuna, let us be thine*
> *own beloved.*

The Rig-Veda reaches its philosophical peak in the "Hymn of Creation," which contains the first mention of a universal spirit.

> *Then there was neither being nor*
> *non-being:*
> *There was no air, nor firmament*
> *beyond it.*
> *Was there a stirring? Where? Beneath*
> *what cover?*
> *Was there a great abyss of unplumbed*
> *water?*
>
> *There was no death nor anything*
> *immortal;*
> *Nor any sign dividing day from night.*
> *That One Thing, in the stillness, breathed*
> *quiescent;*

No second thing existed whatsoever.

*Darkness was hidden in a deeper
    darkness;*
*This All was as a sea without
    dimensions;*
*The void still held unformed what was
    potential,*
*Until the power of Warmth produced
    the sole One . . .*

*Who truly knows, and who can here
    declare it?*
*Whence It was born, and how this world
    was fashioned?*
*The gods came later than the earth's
    creation:*
*Who knows then out of what the world
    has issued?*

*Whether he made the world or did not
    make it,*
*He knows whence this creation came, he
    only*
*Who in the highest heaven guards and
    watches;*
*He knows indeed, but then, perhaps,
    he knows not!*

The fundamental tenets of Hinduism took shape during the three or four centuries after about 800 B.C. They were set down in a series of treatises called the *Upanishads*. The *Upanishads* left some great issues unsettled. The individual Hindu is still free to decide whether he believes the one Supreme Reality is an impersonal essence or spirit, hence to be called Brahman (neuter), or a personal God, hence to be called Brahma (masculine). Similarly the believer may decide that the world is one aspect of Brahman or Brahma, or that it is simply Its or His creation—or he may remain undecided.

In either case, the devout Hindu regards the visible world as *maya*. Like the English word "magic," the Sanskrit *maya* is often translated as "illusion," and many a Westerner has concluded therefrom that the Hindu believes the visible world to be a nonexistent hallucination. What the Hindu actually means is that the world is not simply what it seems to the human senses—a view with which 20th Century western scientists wholly agree. (Although the Greek philosopher Democritus is generally credited with originating the concept of the atom, Hindu thinkers preceded him.)

SINCE the visible world includes human beings, it follows logically that they too are not what they seem. Each man thinks of himself as a separate and unique individual, and each man is obsessed with his personal opinions, desires, pleasures, pains, fears and frustrations. This preoccupation with the outer self, says Hindu philosophy, is the true source of all human evil and misery. Buried deep within every human being, under many layers, is each man's true Self. That Self is *Atman*, the omnipresent, universal soul.

Here again devout Hindus may differ in precise interpretation. One, coldly intellectual, may consider himself no more truly individual than "a drop of spray cast up by a breaking ocean wave." Another, more warm-hearted, may incline toward the Christian view of the immanent God or *Atman* as a universal, ubiquitous spirit, within and yet distinct from the human person. Yet both believers agree that eternal union with God or *Atman* is the supreme goal and destiny of human beings.

Hindus call such mystical union *samadhi* or *moksha*. Another name, used in the *Upanishads* and adopted by Buddha, is *nirvana*. Because *nirvana* literally means "to extinguish" or "to blow out," many Westerners have supposed that the despairing goal of the Hindu and his Buddhist cousin is the cessation of existence, a descent into unknowing, unfeeling blackness. Rather, what is to be extinguished is only the false self which concentrates on the world and the flesh. In the *Upanishads*, *nirvana* is defined as the state of ecstasy attained when the true Self finally realizes its identity with *Atman*. Buddha, who resisted metaphysical discussion in his absorption with problems of the here and now, consistently described the state of *nirvana* as "incomprehensible, indescribable, inconceivable, unutterable." His only affirmative definition: "*Nirvana* is bliss."

Unlike the Judaeo-Christian paradise, *nirvana* can be achieved in this life. Like the 18th and 19th Century rationalists of the West—among them the signers of the Declaration of Independence—Hindus believe that human life and happiness are governed by a natural moral law, inherent in human nature. They agree that a man's every thought and act shapes his character, and they believe also in total free will; for the pious Hindu there is no such thing as accident or chance. But Hindu belief goes far beyond western concepts. *Karma* means "deeds" —mental as well as physical. The Law of *Karma* —impersonal, inexorable, self-enforcing—holds every human being to unforgiving account for every one of his earthly deeds. After death the soul may dwell for a time in a heaven or hell. Then it will be reborn according to the sum of the deeds in all of its previous existences. If the balance of these deeds should be evil, the soul will be reborn as a member of a lower caste, or even as an animal, an insect or a vegetable. If the balance should fall toward the good, the soul will be reborn in a higher caste, or advance toward the attainment of true humanity. In such a state, the reborn being may fleetingly attain *nirvana* in brief union with the eternal. But only final union with God can break the otherwise endless cycle of birth and rebirth.

IT was through the precepts of *karma* and reincarnation that India's caste system became fixed within its dominant religious system, so that violations of caste were rankest heresy. By the Sixth Century B.C., caste barriers had begun to harden and Hinduism was in a state of decay. Members of its priestly caste, called Brahmins, kept most of their wisdom to themselves and offered their followers little but empty ritual and demands for costly sacrifices. In their murky teaching, most humans seemed doomed to an endless cycle of reincarnation.

Two leaders of religious revolt arose within a few years of each other in this period, each offering a clear-cut path to salvation in this life. The first was the founder of Jainism, Nataputta Vardhamana, called Mahavira (the great hero) and Jina (the victor). He taught that the false self and its desires can be crushed and *nirvana* attained by right living and asceticism. A major item in Jina's ethical creed was *ahimsa*, meaning noninjury to any living creature. His present-day followers, naked or clad only in loincloth, still wear cloths over their mouths lest they accidentally inhale an insect. Vegetarians, they avoid injury to living vegetables by waiting until someone else has cooked them, then beg for the leftovers.

THE second and greater of the rebel leaders was Siddhartha Gautama, called Buddha (the enlightened one), one of the great spiritual leaders of all time. Legend says that he was the son of a king of a state in northern India and that he was sheltered from all sight of human misery until early manhood. When he encountered it at last, he abandoned his wealth, wife and child, and went wandering in search of enlightenment. After learning all he could from Hindu holy men, he tried asceticism—going unwashed until the dirt fell from him in cakes, almost dying of starvation. Meditating under the Bo tree, he found what he was seeking. All life, he realized, involves suffering. The cause of suffering is desire. When desire is quenched, suffering ceases and the soul achieves *nirvana*. For attainment of this end, Buddha prescribed a high ethical code, but—without mention of a deity—placed his main reliance on meditation and mental self-discipline rather than on asceticism. He retained many doctrines of Hinduism. Founding an order of monks, he set an example of serene wisdom and compassion throughout his life. Buddhism flourished in India for a thousand years after his death.

Then Hinduism began to display its eclectic genius. Hindus have long believed that God periodically comes to earth in the form of a human person, called an *avatar*. Many Hindus accept Jesus Christ and Mohammed as such. In the *Bhagavad-Gita*, a brief religious classic which some 2,000 years ago was made part of the enormous religious epic called the *Maha-bharata*, one such *avatar*, Krishna, declaims these lines to his suffering human companion:

> *When goodness grows weak,*
> *When evil increases,*
> *I make myself a body.*
> *In every age I come back*
> *To deliver the holy,*
> *To destroy the sin of the sinner,*
> *To establish the righteous.*

Buddha was enshrined as an *avatar* in the Hindu pantheon—as odd a development as Martin Luther's sanctification by the Roman Catholic Church would be—and his doctrine of the quenching of desire came to be adopted as a Hindu tenet. Jainism's *ahimsa* was also absorbed. Thus the two protestant heresies, far from injuring Hinduism, reformed and clarified and strengthened it.

In his superb work, *The Religions of Man*, Professor Huston Smith of the Massachusetts Institute of Technology writes: "If we were to take Hinduism as a whole—its vast literature, its opulent art, its elaborate rituals, its sprawling folkways—if we were to take this enormous outlook in its entirety and epitomize it in a single, central affirmation we would find it saying to man: 'You can have what you want.' "

Hinduism, which insists on assaying human nature not only for what it could be but for what it is, lists the primary wants of ordinary man as pleasure and worldly success—wealth, fame, power. It declares that, taken honestly and in moderation and with due regard for the rights of others, there is nothing whatever wrong with these objectives. They are as desirable for most adults as toys are for most children. But in time such desires, like toys, are outgrown—if not in one lifetime, then in some future incarnation. Sooner or later, in this or some future incarnation, a man finds himself restless and unsatisfied.

He then proceeds to another objective—the satisfaction of service to his community and fellow men. This is a nobler and more mature desire, yet in time man discovers that it too is

not enough. As long as a human being's true identity remains buried and unrealized, as long as he wanders through the world like a king stricken with amnesia wandering through his kingdom, his dissatisfaction and disquietude will continue.

Man's final desire springs from his possession of a divine and immortal soul. That soul, which is the true person, will never be satisfied, Hinduism says, with less than three ultimate attainments. The first is infinite existence, eternal life. The only man who truly welcomes mortal death is the one who is confident that he is only passing on to a higher stage of life. Second, the soul desires infinite knowledge. Mystery tantalizes a man, ignorance gnaws at him, lack of understanding frustrates him, discovery exhilarates him. Third, the soul looks for infinite joy—that happiness, far beyond the pleasures afforded by gratification of the senses, that comes with full realization of the true Self.

These ultimate objectives, Hinduism says, can be attained only through union with God.

THERE are different ways to attain this divine union. Hinduism divides people into four basic types: reflective, emotional, active and experimental. To each of these groups Hinduism offers a technique—a yoga—for approaching God. Since few people are exclusively of one type, the techniques may be combined according to individual preference.

"Yoga," deriving from the same root as the English "yoke," carries the same double meaning: to harness or discipline (under the yoke), and to unite (yoke with). The word is loosely applied to any program or technique which leads toward the union with God. More specifically, and as it is generally understood in the West, yoga refers to a technique of physical and mental self-discipline achieved through various exercises and postures. The practitioner is called a yogi. There are several types of such yogas, including one, *hatha yoga*, which concentrates, for all practical purposes, solely on physical culture. India is full of showmen—yogis who delight their audiences with such astonishing feats as bringing up their intestines, popping out their eyeballs and rolling them on their cheeks, and, apparently through power to stop or slow their heartbeats and breathing, allowing themselves to be buried alive. But the original and still primary purpose of such mastery of the body is not to attract attention but to banish the distractions of habit and desire that interfere with the possibility of divine communion.

Less well-known are the nonphysical yogas. The Way of Knowledge, known as *jnana yoga*, is intended for practitioners who are primarily reflective. Its disciples seek their identity with *Atman* through pure reason. The student begins with a perusal of Hindu scriptures and other religious lore. This stage is followed by prolonged meditation on the lessons learned. Eventually, the student begins to concentrate solely on the identity of the eternal Spirit and the true Self; as a means to that end he is encouraged to think of himself in the third person.

The Way of Love, or *bhakti yoga*, for persons who are primarily emotional, is by far the most popular of the yoga techniques. To a degree it resembles Christian practice. To men who are unable to grasp or be satisfied with abstract concepts, it offers the aids of image, ritual, repetitive prayer and devotion to a favorite *avatar* or some other more humanly understandable manifestation of the Supreme Reality. Of the many gods in the Hindu pantheon, three are held universally supreme: Brahma, the Creator; Vishnu, the Preserver; and Shiva, the Destroyer. The followers of Shiva and Vishnu form the largest of the Hindu sects. As a counter to possible accusations of idolatry and polytheism the following invocation is offered by priests in the temples which are dedicated to them and to the numberless other gods who represent the varying attributes of the Absolute in Hindu theology:

> O Lord, forgive three sins that are due to
>   my human limitations:
> Thou art everywhere, but I worship you here;
> Thou art without form, but I worship you in
>   these forms;
> Thou needest no praise, yet I offer you
>   these prayers and salutations.
> Lord, forgive three sins that are due to
>   my human limitations.

The Way of Work, or *karma yoga*, is for those who are primarily active. It assures its followers that they need not abandon the world in order to find God. The only change required is one of mental attitude. Whether the work of the follower by simple manual labor or high political leadership, he must forget all thought of himself, caring nothing for personal success or failure but seeking only to serve God. Mohandas K. Gandhi, the dedicated little man whose abhorrence of self, success and violence was finally to set India on the road to independence (see Chapter 5), was the country's greatest exemplar of the Way of Work.

The Way of Mystical Experience (*rajah yoga*) appeals to those who are primarily experimental. Like the Way of Knowledge, it is open only to the few who have the capacity and the will for it. It, too, sometimes employs physical techniques. Anyone may learn some of the elementary exercises and postures as an aid to health and meditation. But the would-be yogi normally begins his training in early youth and spends years in mastering the necessary disciplines. He must begin with five desire-killing vows and five self-disciplinary

THE SACRED COW

The Hindu veneration for the cow dates back at least 3,000 years and may have originated partly as a practical measure to protect the supply of milk. Eventually the custom became ingrained in religious tradition. Cows are not actually worshiped as deities in India and many of them are not especially well treated. In practice the veneration takes the form of an absolute prohibition against killing a cow. The animal's products are often used in Hindu religious rites.

rules: to abstain from harming any living thing, from deceit, theft, greed and unchastity; to study, to pray, to practice cleanliness, calm and mortification. In western eyes, some of the yogi's postures and exercises—such as learning to breathe in one nostril and out the other—seem freakish. But all of them are the product of many centuries of experiment and experience. All of the physical techniques, yogis believe, lead toward the self-mastery required for union with God.

MASTERY of the body and of its distracting desires for a drink, a cigarette, a stretch or even a scratch is only a step toward mastery of the mind. Fond of metaphor and simile, Hindus compare the tendency of the undisciplined mind to leap from one thought or memory or sensation to another, to a crazed monkey leaping around its cage. Unsatisfied, they move toward sharper definition by comparing the undisciplined mind to a crazed, drunken monkey leaping around its cage; a crazed, drunken monkey with St. Vitus' dance; a crazed, drunken monkey with St. Vitus' dance that has just been stung by a wasp.

As a step toward mind control, the apprentice yogi practices concentration on a single thought or mental image. The final step is to banish all thought as well as all sensation and, thus free of all earthly bonds, to wait for the *Atman* to make itself known. Not every aspirant attains the goal of mystical union, and the attempt—especially for those who try without a teacher—involves danger of physical or psychic injury. But those who succeed insist, like mystics everywhere, that the mystical experience is one of incomparable ecstasy.

There was neither defiance nor arrogance in the message which the Indian holy men sent to Alexander the Great. All mystics agree that the mystical union cannot be adequately described; it must be experienced. One who has not experienced it may reasonably doubt its reality. How does it differ from an hallucination?

Except perhaps to leave him more addled than before, an hallucination or a delusion does not change its victim. In all times and countries, mystics and those acquainted with them have testified that the mystical experience seems to transform the character of one who has undergone it. The genuine mystic indisputably possesses a matchless serenity and wisdom, and an overflowing compassion and a dedication to good works.

A westerner visited one of India's greatest modern yogis, Sri Ramana Maharshi, shortly before Sri Ramana's death in 1950. "Sri Ramana would have looked like a superior human being in any surroundings," he wrote. "He had the quietly assured look of a man who has experienced a great deal and thought everything through to a final, unshakable conclusion. Even an unbeliever could see that he possessed a sort of personal serenity that is rare even in the contemplative Orient." Said one of Sri Ramana's disciples, a former professor of English literature: "You can attain peace merely by being near him."

THE approach to such serenity is of course not easy. For the male Hindu with the will and means, life is divided into four stages. First, beginning with the rite of initiation between the ages of eight and 12 and lasting by tradition for 12 years, comes life as a student. With marriage, the student becomes a householder, enjoying the pleasures of the senses and of family life, seeking worldly success and serving his community and fellow men. At any time after the birth of his first grandchild he is free to cast off these pleasures and responsibilities and, after providing for his wife if she does not care to come with him, retire to the forest in search of enlightenment. When this quest has succeeded, he enters his final earthly state as a *sannyasin* or holy man, a homeless beggar possessing nothing but a loincloth and an alms bowl. "Taking no thought of the future and looking with indifference upon the present," says one Hindu text, the *sannyasin* "lives identified with the eternal Self and beholds nothing else." Many Hindus find it difficult to believe that Christian missionaries, enjoying such luxuries as shoes and houses and regular meals, can be genuine holy men.

From the sublime expression of religion in the lives of genuine yogis and *sannyasins* to that same religion's expression in the present-day caste system is a long step downward. The Sanskrit word for caste is *varna*, meaning "color," and the system presumably originated with the ancient Aryans' conquest of the subcontinent's black-skinned aborigines and dark-complexioned Dravidians. Division of labor, sanitation and other factors may also have been involved. The system divides Hindus into four major castes. In descending order, they are: Brahmins, priests and intellectuals; Kshatriyas, aristocrats and warriors; Vaishyas, merchants and farmers; Shudras, menials. The four castes are in turn divided into some 3,000 subcastes, each with its own status, traditions, rules and regulations. The most stringent caste rules prohibit marriage, dining or other social contact outside one's caste. Technically outside the caste system altogether (though they have formed castes of their own) are some 50 million outcastes or Untouchables, whose very shadow may defile a caste Hindu.

ALTHOUGH divisive and depressing to non-Hindus, the caste system is neither senseless nor wholly cruel. Even before untouchability was outlawed in 1948, Untouchables were not slaves, and those Untouchables who renounced the world for God were revered, like all *sannyasins*, as above caste. Caste privileges entail comparable responsibilities. Punishment for a crime is far heavier for a member of a high caste than for a low-caste or outcaste. Each caste and subcaste may freely make its own rules and each has its own sphere of work in which outsiders may not compete. Like medieval feudalism, the caste system makes for a stable, orderly society.

Also like feudalism, however, it makes for a static society. By requiring every man to remain in the station and occupation to which he is born, it dams the upward flow of talent. And by fencing off Indians from each other, it often impedes social and economic progress.

Prime Minister Jawaharlal Nehru, a non-practicing Brahmin, and other politicians, intellectuals and businessmen who are striving to lead India out of its ancient poverty have excellent practical reasons for seeking to modernize not only the caste system but the religion in which it is embedded. Hinduism holds that world progress is both improbable and evanescent. Even if the world should become a much better place than it has always been, which he doubts, the pious Hindu believes that it would only have to be done all over again. His religion teaches that the universe itself periodically dies and is reincarnated to repeat the whole cycle of its previous existences.

SPECIFIC obstacles to progress abound in Hindu practice and belief. *Ahisma*, the respect for life, is carried to what westerners consider wasteful and destructive extremes in the special protection afforded to cows and to monkeys. Efforts to control India's burgeoning population are hampered by the Hindu's belief that his soul is likely to remain in a hell indefinitely unless he leaves children to pray for his swift reincarnation.

Today, caste lines are weakening under the necessities of independence and of modern transportation and industry, the impact of education, the laws against untouchability, the reservation of certain government jobs for Untouchables, the rebellion of some women against the ancient bonds of their inferior status. Nevertheless millions of Hindus still cling stubbornly to the caste system and to their religion as a whole.

Thus one of the great human experiments of history proceeds. If India can find a way to attain a fair degree of material prosperity and equality of opportunity without loss of its spiritual riches, it is conceivable that—at least to the extent of teaching lessons that may be applied to western conditions and beliefs—the 21st Century possibility which Arnold Toynbee suggested in 1952 may come to pass: "India the conquered will conquer its conquerors."

CASTE INITIATE, a boy performs with his father the sacred thread ceremony (*right*) which will confirm him as a full-fledged member of one of the three highest castes.

The Countless Faces of Piety

In Hinduism there are no universal rules for the orthodox. A Hindu's caste, his region, the star under which he was born, the sect he chooses and the god he favors all combine to shape the rules he follows. If a Brahmin he must study the Vedas; if a member of a low caste he is forbidden to read them. If he worships Vishnu he may eat meat, but if he worships Shiva he considers eating meat a sin. In the Carnatic region a lower-caste Sudra drinks liquor, but a Brahmin may not. In actual practice, the religion that binds a subcontinent may be as unique to an individual Hindu as his face.

FERVENT FILE, Jains mount the holy hill of Vindhyagiri (*left*) to pay homage to an idol enshrined on the hilltop. The Jains are forbidden to kill any living thing.

ANOINTED IDOL, the 57-foot-high statue of the Jain god Gotmateswara (*opposite*) receives a vegetarian's tribute of vermilion, oil, poppies and mashed bananas.

LIFELIKE FIGURES, multi-colored statues illustrate episodes in the life of the Hindu god Shiva on this Madras tower. Mounted on a temple gate, it displays 800 representations of the deity, of his kinsmen and of other gods.

SACRED RIVER, the Ganges
is believed by many Hindus to be
a goddess. The river is said
to bring purity, wealth and fertility
to those who bathe in it

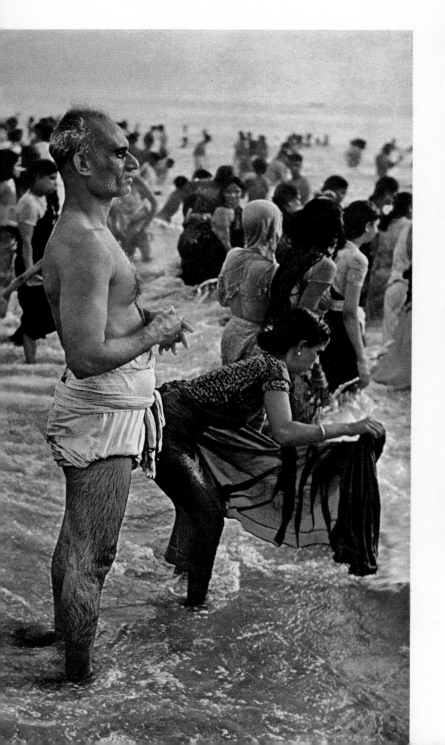

HOPEFUL PILGRIMS wade in the Ganges (*left*). Believers in reincarnation, many Hindus come here to die in hopes of attaining higher status in their future lives.

MASS IMMERSIONS reach a peak during the celebration of the ritual of *Kumbh Mela*, when four million bathers crowd the juncture of the Ganges and Jumna Rivers, thought by many Hindus to be the holiest place in the world. At one *Kumbh Mela*, 500 persons were crushed to death when the signal was sounded to start the bathing.

SIKHS prepare holy water (*left*) to initiate four men into their sect. Sikhism has some 6.2 million adherents, concentrated primarily in the Punjab.

CHRISTIANS attend services barefoot (*opposite*), following Indian custom. Many of India's 8.2 million Christians come from the Untouchable ranks.

3

The Half-Forgotten Past

THERE is little Indian political history that is innately felt or systematically ordered by Indians themselves. Specific names, places, dates, epochs and empires which the world and the Indians know of that history have generally been recorded by foreign observers or dug up, long afterward, by foreign scholars. Onesicritus, the young officer who accompanied Alexander the Great to India, was one of the first chroniclers of Indian actuality, and it remained for 19th Century European scholars, for example, to piece together something of the story of Ashoka, ancient India's greatest emperor, who reigned from 273 to 232 B.C.

The Indian past conforms to Matthew Arnold's celebrated image of

> . . . *a darkling plain,*
> *Swept with confused alarums of struggle and*
> *flight*
> *Where ignorant armies clash by night.*

Out of the fogged and half-forgotten Indian past, phantoms of civilizations, men and empires arise, like misted plains, peaks and plateaus. Indian history is punctuated by these high points; indeed, they supply one of the few real clues to an understanding of the nation's early days. For while western history generally appears to observers as linear—a more or less purposeful progression from Greece and Rome and the founding of Christianity down to the present day—the Indian story is cyclical. Chaos and order alternate with striking regularity, and in the recurring fluctuations from one to the other the same figures seem to reappear in the same roles.

THE oldest civilization of India was the Dravidian. Its unity rested on language rather than race. Dravidian civilization embraced the original inhabitants of India, black-skinned people similar to African Negroes. Some of them were small, primitive forest dwellers; others were taller and more progressive denizens of the plains. With them mingled the Veddids and the Melanids, who came along later. The Veddids came from lands to the north of India, and some of them were rather light-skinned with curly hair. The Melanids were a brown people whose exact geographic origin is still unsettled.

One of the finest monuments of the ancient civilization is a city recently uncovered by archaeologists at Mohenjo-Daro in the Indus Valley in northwest India. Mohenjo-Daro was a city with wide streets, public baths and several-storied houses complete with bathrooms. Its citizens left behind splendid pottery, bronze tools, silver beakers and gold jewelry. They also handed down a handsome picture script that to this day has defied deciphering.

The Aryans poured into India about 2000 B.C., defeating the ancient Dravidian civilization and making the most lasting imprint of any race on the country. They probably originated in central Europe and entered Asia by way of Persia. They were tall and fair, racially arrogant, heroically warlike and cunning in their infiltration of the advanced Dravidian civilization. The Aryans continued to penetrate Indian life, thought and literature for a millennium known as the Vedic period, whose hymns and other sacred writings are called the Vedas.

The most profound Aryan impact on Indian life took place in two domains: language and the caste system. Today Dravidian languages—Telugu, Kanarese, Malayalam and Tamil—are spoken only in the southernmost part of India. Aryan languages, derived from the same source as Sanskrit, are used in all the rest of the country.

India's caste system obtained religious sanction under the Aryans and may have been based initially on color and race. The Aryans resisted intermarriage, and in Sanskrit the word for color and caste is the same, *varna*. But in time the Aryans inevitably intermingled with the Indian peoples they conquered. Then caste became based on social position as well as race (see Chapter 2). Today India's caste system testifies to a popular instinct for social immobility and rigidity that is unmatched in any other civilization.

As Aryan power in northern India waned, it receded to the east. The Persians dominated northwest India, exacting immense tribute and raising Indian levies for their wars against the Greeks. When the Greeks overcame the Persians, Alexander the Great bore the borders of his empire deep into India until his wearied troops refused to cross the River Beas.

THE first great identifiable personage in Indian political history is the emperor Chandragupta Maurya. He was a military leader in the Kingdom of Magadha on the Ganges in eastern India. Magadha was consolidating and expanding its power in north central India while the northwest was crumbling before the Greek invaders. Chandragupta, advised by a Brahmin named Chanakya, who is often called the Indian Machiavelli, shrewdly exploited this situation to establish his own power.

Chandragupta went to Alexander the Great while he was still in India, probably in 325 B.C., and urged him to invade Magadha, depose the king and leave Chandragupta in control. This plan came to naught. But after Alexander died, Chandragupta took a different tack to achieve his ambition. He incited a popular uprising in the Punjab, expelled the Greeks and used his Punjab allies to overrun Magadha and to install himself as king.

He did not rest on his laurels. When Alexander's successor in Asia, Seleucus Nicator, tried to reconquer the Punjab, Chandragupta defeated him and pushed Magadha's boundaries all the way across northern India to the passes of Afghanistan. In return for a Greek promise to leave India to him, Chandragupta conceded that Persia would be a Greek sphere of influence.

A revealing account of the way Chandragupta lived and reigned was left by Megasthenes, the Greek ambassador at the powerful Indian monarch's court in Pataliputra (modern Patna). Chandragupta was a full-fledged dictator—pompous, cruel and constantly fearful for his life. When he left the palace, which was seldom, he proceeded in great state and under elaborate guard. As he rode on a litter atop an elephant he was surrounded by a multitude of attendants pulling cages containing buffaloes, lions and leopards, or carrying jewel-encrusted copper drinking vessels and golden goblets. His bodyguard of Amazons held back the crowds, and ". . . it was death to come inside the line of women." Back in the palace—a massive structure of carved wood plated with gold and silver—Chandragupta reveled among slave girls who played music and danced for him. But he had all his food tested for poison, slept in a different bedroom every night and filled the palace and the capital with spies to protect him from assassination.

IN his ruthlessness, Chandragupta enslaved his subjects and executed any enemy that reared its head. He ruled with a cold efficiency, building a network of roads, creating vast irrigation schemes and exploiting the mines and forests for the state's benefit. With his huge revenues, especially from the land (all of which was owned by the state), he maintained a large army complete with chariots and elephants.

Chandragupta died or killed himself about 298 B.C. His son Bindusara succeeded him for a quarter of a century and enlarged the Mauryan Empire by substantial conquests in the central part of India.

Bindusara's son Ashoka, who ascended the throne in 273 B.C., at first behaved like his father and grandfather, ruthlessly expanding his domain. He decided to enlarge his central Indian empire and invaded what is now Orissa. The Orissans fiercely stood their ground against Ashoka's depredations, and the resulting war was terrible. A hundred thousand fell in battle, many more died from famine and disease, and 125,000 prisoners were taken before Ashoka gained his awful victory and consolidated his vast empire.

THEN a great change came over Ashoka, a change distantly akin to the later conversion of Paul on the road to Damascus. A celebrated Buddhist sage, Upagupta, won Ashoka's confidence and showed him the evil of unbridled violence. Ashoka was converted to Buddhism, repented of his ambition and cruelty and became a ruler of piety and peace.

Henceforth Ashoka governed according to the Buddhist *Dharma*, or Law of Piety. "The only true victory is that effected by the Law," he declared. "The conquest of the Law alone is a conquest full of delight." He interpreted the Law, in terms as simple and popular as those of the Ten Commandments, to mean "hearkening to elders, reverence to the aged, and seemly treatment of Brahmins and ascetics, of the poor and wretched, yea, even of slaves and servants." These precepts were not merely nostrums for the people, but standards for the government itself. "Work I must, for the welfare of all the folk," Ashoka said.

To make known his principles, Ashoka had them engraved on rocks and pillars throughout his kingdom. (From these inscriptions scholars have reconstructed the story of his reign.) He matched his deeds to his words by repealing oppressive laws, pardoning prisoners and reducing the wanton slaughter of animals for sacrifices. On the more positive side, he promoted the material well-being, health and education of his subjects.

Ashoka's greatest achievement was the wide diffusion of Buddhism. He enjoined complete religious tolerance, and even officially support-ed other sects, but the bulk of his encourage-ment went to the propagators of his own faith. He himself made a pilgrimage to the Holy Places of Buddhism. He converted the army of spies whom he had inherited into "Overseers of the Law," who were required to report on the prog-ress of religion in their various districts. Most important, he sent Buddhist missionaries to the northernmost and southernmost parts of India, which he had not conquered by the sword, and to Ceylon and Burma.

The missionaries not only implanted the or-derly principles and moral precepts of Bud-dhism but carried with them the culture and civilization of Ashoka's realm. Ashoka advanced Buddhism from the role of a sect to that of a mighty religion.

After a reign of more than 40 years, Ashoka died in 232 B.C. For reasons that are buried in obscurity, the Mauryan Empire soon followed him to the grave. Its last ruler was assassinated in 185 B.C. A reaction to Ashoka's rule set in, animal sacrifice was revived, the Buddhists were persecuted and the subcontinent disinte-grated into warring states, beset by invaders from Central Asia.

SO ended one of the classic cycles of Indian history. A people called the Kushans, part of a nomadic horde from China, entered India from the northwest sometime in the Second or First Century B.C. and began to dominate the country. Gradually they conquered the Punjab, Sind and some of central India, and pushed east to take over the northern India area that Chandragupta and Magadha had controlled.

The only Kushan ruler about whom much is known was Kanishka, who probably occupied his throne in what is now Peshawar in northwest India from 120 to 162 A.D. To Kanishka and his tall, bearded followers, India was merely a conquered foreign territory, while Central Asia was their homeland. They hated India's hot cli-mate, they stuck to their native padded coats and riding boots and they summered in the cooler Kashmir and Afghanistan. The Kushans

felt an affinity for the imperial Romans who had penetrated into Asia Minor, exchanging ambassadors with them, trading with them and copying their coinage.

A special work of Kanishka's foreignness was his embracing of Buddhism at a time when Hinduism was vigorously on the rise in India. Buddhism seemed relatively simple and direct to Kanishka, like a general doctrine of salvation in which he could forgive as a secular savior. He called a General Council of Buddhists in Kashmir and ordered the conclusions of the council to be engraved on copper sheets that have yet to be unearthed. But meanwhile Hin-duism was spinning an intricate web of beliefs and social doctrines that reflected native life and probably constituted a protest of the In-dian people against their foreign conquerors.

ACCORDING to Indian legend, Kanishka's death in 162 was resolved by the people. The story goes that people were saying to each other, in effect, "The King is greedy, cruel and unreasonable. His campaigns and continued conquests have wearied the mass of his servants. We must agree among ourselves and get rid of him. After that we may be happy." Kanishka was smothered under a quilt.

After Kanishka's death, a feeling possibly akin to modern nationalism came into play against the invaders, leading to their expulsion and to the establishment of the Hindu Gupta Empire. An Indian leader of obscure origin exploited this sentiment by taking the historic name of Chandragupta and installing himself in the original Chandragupta's erstwhile capi-tal, Pataliputra. In one of the most dramatic manifestations of the cyclical effect in Indian history, the new Chandragupta founded a dy-nasty whose course more or less duplicated that of his namesake: the first two emperors were conquerors while the third, Chandragupta II, imitated Ashoka by being first a warrior and then a man of peace. Chandragupta conquered much of northern India, his son Samudragupta extended the empire southward, and Chandra-gupta II, before his conversion to mildness, carried Gupta power far into western India.

Chandragupta II in his later years was a model of justice, mercy and efficiency in government. Fa Hsien, a Chinese pilgrim, has left an account of life under the ruler. Chandragupta II promoted religious devotion to Hinduism just as Ashoka had promoted Buddhism. Again like Ashoka, Chandragupta II stood for religious tolerance, and the Brahmins were notably generous to Buddhist priests. Chandragupta II also saw to it that the economy prospered and that the people were liberally supplied with social services. He died in 415, after a reign of 35 years.

As the Mauryan Empire had fallen soon after the death of Ashoka, so Gupta power dissolved after the passing of Chandragupta II. The foreign invaders came again. White Huns from Central Asia overran northwestern India and pressed toward the eastern part. Legend has it that a century of sporadic terror ensued. One of the Hun chieftains, Toramana, had some of the redeeming features of a buccaneer: he was a hardy fighter who could be magnanimous. But his son Mihiragula was a madman of the same destructive variety as the fabled Attila. Mihiragula delighted in desecrating religious shrines, massacring priests and peaceful citizens, and watching the death agonies of elephants that had been pushed from precipices for the gratification of his pleasure.

ONCE more, the outraged Indian nationalists reacted. An alliance of Hindu princes drove Mihiragula into Kashmir and destroyed Hun power in 528. However, the departure of the Huns did not bring peace and order to India. For decades, the manifold Hindu states quarreled and fought with each other.

Order eventually returned to India with the reign of Harsha from 606 to 647. During Harsha's childhood, three states had dominated the Ganges valley. At the age of 16, Harsha was called to the throne of Thanesar, north of modern Delhi, which was vacant because of dark incidents of treachery and assassination. Skilled in war, Harsha conquered surrounding territories, uniting the contending sovereignties and going on to consolidate much of India north of the Vindhya Mountains.

Like Ashoka and Chandragupta II before him, Harsha was religiously tolerant, merciful and competent as a ruler. He leaned toward Buddhism but did not discriminate against the Hindu Brahmins. "In all the highways of the towns and villages throughout India," one memorial of his reign notes, "he erected hospices, provided food and drink and stationed there physicians with medicines for travellers and poor persons round about, to be given without stint." And he was "an indefatigable worker and the day was too short for him."

Hiuen Tsang, a Chinese Buddhist scholar who arrived in India in 630, was Harsha's leading eulogist. Hiuen Tsang described the ruler thus: "His skill in literature was profound. . . . From the time of his birth to his last hour, his face never crimsoned with anger, nor did his hands ever injure a living thing. During the fifty and more years of his reign, the wild beasts became familiar with men and the people did not injure or slay them. Such were his love and humanity."

This view of Harsha idealized not only him but also the relatively tranquil decades that he dominated. Exaggerated as it was, the idealization had an undertone of "Let's enjoy it while it lasts"—a presentiment that the relatively decent rule of Harsha would soon be followed by a new night. Indeed, this did occur. For nearly two centuries after Harsha's death, fresh chaos and confusion beset India.

THE belligerent Rajputs ("Sons of Kings") sprang into prominence in the 9th Century. The Rajput rulers were descended from Central Asian invaders who had assimilated with the Hindus. They took on the Hindu faith, invented purely Indian family trees for themselves and even claimed ancestral membership in the Kshatriya, or warrior, caste. The Rajputs provided India with a rough facsimile of European feudalism. They were clannish, proud and poetic, and they were quite content to rule over limited sovereignties. None of them really aspired to all-Indian power as past emperors had done. Provincial lordship was enough.

This made the Rajputs relatively easy picking for the centralized and disciplined power of Islamic leaders when they turned their acquisitive attention toward India in the 11th Century. Mahmud of Ghazni, a Central Asian operating out of Afghanistan, invaded India no less than 17 times, routed the Rajputs in every raid and carried away immense booty. Mahmud's most notorious foray took him into the resplendent Hindu temple of Somnath. There, as elephants trumpeted, dancing girls shrieked and Brahmins wailed entreaties, he stalked into the innermost shrine of the temple. Swinging his heavy mace, he smashed to smithereens the great idol of Shiva and " . . . out gushed a store of rubies like splinters of ice, and emeralds like sprays of myrtle, and pearls as big as pigeons' eggs."

THE Moslem Muhammed Ghori, who succeeded to power in Afghanistan, was more systematic than Mahmud. He was not content with raids and brigandage, but stationed his general Kutb-ud-din Ibak in Delhi with orders to subjugate all of India. Early in the 13th Century, Kutb-ud-din Ibak controlled the bulk of northern India and proclaimed himself Sultan of Delhi. This was the formal inauguration of Moslem rule, which in due course spread over most of India and which, with various undercuttings, interruptions and alterations, was to last until the 19th Century.

The Delhi sultanate, once established, was subject to the same intrigue, incompetence, civil war and invasion as many previous Indian regimes. Resentful Hindu potentates attacked it from within India. Genghis Khan threatened it from without, but halted his advance at the Indus River. Tamerlane was less reticent: sweeping down from Samarkand, he sacked Delhi in 1398 and crippled the sultanate forever. After Tamerlane's invasion, an observer wrote, "For two whole months, not a bird moved a wing in the city."

Moslem rule flourished under other auspices. In 1525, a Moslem descendant of both Genghis Khan and Tamerlane named Babur came out of Kabul in Afghanistan to confront the Sultan of Delhi. Their armies faced each other on the field of Panipat. Babur's force was only one third the size of the sultan's, but the invader had a new and dreadful weapon—artillery. At the first salvo from Babur's side, the sultan's elephants turned and ran, trampling troops and spreading panic on their way. The sultan and 20,000 of his men were slain in the battle of Panipat. Babur occupied Delhi and in the five succeeding years before his death overran most of northern India.

Babur "laid the first stone of the splendid fabric" of the so-called Mogul Empire, which reached its peak in the reign of Babur's grandson, the great Akbar. Akbar came to the throne in 1556, when he was only 14. By the time he was 35, he had extended his realm to reach from the borders of Central Asia to Assam in the east, and from the Himalayas to the Vindhya Mountains. After spending the first 21 years of his reign building his empire, Akbar devoted the last 28 years to administering it with justice, charity and religious tolerance.

DURING the reign of Akbar's son Salim, a wholly new breed of foreign conquerors knocked at India's portals. Britain's envoys called at the Mogul court to petition the emperor to allow ships of the East India Company to dock and trade at Indian ports. One of these Englishmen was a Captain Hawkins, and there is a legend that he treated Salim's young daughter when she fell sick with a fever. The child recovered, and Salim—who called himself Jahangir, or conqueror of the world—asked Hawkins to name any reward he liked. "I want nothing for myself," Hawkins said, "but I beg your majesty to help my country in trading with yours."

Jahangir consented, in probably the most momentous bargain in the entire Indian past. Forgetful India was now about to embark on a very systematic history.

Carved in the 13th Century, a wall in the temple complex at Konarak shows Hindu gods in infinitely varied postures of dance.

A Noble Antiquity Enduring in Stone

Nothing from the past gives as profound an explanation of the ways and purposes of the ancient Indian peoples as their temples and statuary. The grandeur and lavish detail of the structures reveal an enduring reverence for the Hindu deities. Even oppression of foreign powers did not prevent the Indians from building their shrines. Conquerors could come, but the gods, carved in stone, danced and held in their exotic sway the loyalty of the people.

55

HUGE TEMPLE at Ellora, Kailasa was hewn by Hindus in the 8th Century out of the rock that originally filled the site.

HOLY CAVE in a hillside near the temple enshrines Shiva and his courtiers (*center*) and the Seven Hindu Mothers (*right*).

MONUMENTAL SHRINE *reveals the painstaking labor and art of the ancients*

ROYAL OBSERVATORY was designed by Jaipur's Maharaja Jai Singh in 1734. The shafts with steps cast shadows for measuring the sun's distance from the equator.

ABSTRACT PATTERN emerges from the huge functional forms of stone (*opposite*) used for measuring such phenomena as the declination of the stars and solar time.

Students at a private boarding school in Andhra Pradesh wear the impeccable white trousers considered mandatory for a proper

A Glorious and Rapacious Era

game of cricket. Two centuries of British dominance created a class of Indians who fervently maintain English ways and attitudes.

ACROSS the huge expanse of India, the trains run efficiently on a railway network laid out by English engineers. In India's courts, in its offices and in its Parliament, the language is English. On green fields in New Delhi, Indian gentlemen cry "Well bowled!" as the cricket ball whizzes past the batsman to strike the wicket. In another city the troops of a crack Indian regiment mass for parade in the harsh sunlight; their top officers sport swagger sticks and bear the unmistakable stamp of Sandhurst, Britain's top military academy.

It is more than a decade since the British officially departed from India. In all probability it will take more than the 300 years that the British spent in the country to erase the marks of their tenure. Theirs was a memorable era on the subcontinent, by turns glorious and inglorious, bloody and serene—a time of rapacious exploitation, of dreadful famine, of incredible heroism and of fantastic pageantry.

Scarcely more than half a century ago, it appeared that the British would remain masters of India forever. It was only in 1902 that Queen

A Glorious and Rapacious Era

Victoria's heir, the aging Edward VII, was crowned king-emperor of one quarter of the earth. The solemn and ancient coronation ceremonial in London, impressive as it was, was dwarfed by the great coronation durbar in Delhi. A multitude of 150,000 visitors swarmed into the city. All of India's princelings, maharajas and nawabs, splendidly costumed and blazing with jewels, had gathered to pay homage to their new and distant monarch. The streets trembled with the heavy tread of elephants and resounded to the cymbals and drums of the massed military bands. In the van of the procession, resplendent inside a silver *howdah* on the back of a bedecked elephant, rode the viceroy himself, the imperious Lord Curzon, later to become one of the most renowned of the empire's diplomats. Beside him Lady Curzon nodded graciously to the king-emperor's subjects. And behind them the great Lord Kitchener, conqueror of the Sudan and already a legend, led some 35,000 Indian and British troops in a stirring and splendid show of military pomp and might.

THE British were lords of the earth, and nowhere was their dominion more apparent than in India, "the brightest jewel" in the imperial diadem. Yet that empire on which the sun never set was already nearing its twilight hour. While all India hailed King Edward, the young lawyer Mohandas Gandhi was already struggling for civil liberties in South Africa, and on an estate in Allahabad a teenaged boy, Jawaharlal Nehru, was absorbing his lessons under the guidance of an Irish tutor.

In 1947, scarcely four decades after the great durbar, Victoria's great-grandson Earl Mountbatten presided as the saffron, white and green tricolor replaced the Union Jack over New Delhi. India was a free and independent nation. With deep emotion the last viceroy read the farewell message of his cousin, King George VI: "Freedom-loving people everywhere will wish to share in your celebrations," he said, "for with this transfer of power by consent comes the fulfillment of a great democratic

ideal. . . . It is inspiring to think that all this has been achieved by means of peaceful change. Heavy responsibilities lie ahead of you, but when I consider the statesmanship you have already shown and the great sacrifices you have already made, I am confident that you will be worthy of your destiny."

THE British did not originally come to India bent on conquest. They came as traders, and they were late on the scene. Unlike the Portuguese, the French and the Dutch, the 17th Century British were not nearly so interested in acquiring Indian pepper, ginger and calico—or Indian territory—as they were in finding a market for their own woolens and metals. Long after Vasco da Gama had discovered the water route from western Europe to India around the southern tip of Africa, British seafarers continued to probe doggedly at the American coast in an effort to find a westward passage to China. Because of its cooler climate, China was considered a better market for British wool than torrid India. It was a century after Da Gama's voyage that an English expedition first ventured into the Indian Ocean, and it was not until 1609 that the British decided to pursue the Indian trade in earnest. James I graciously renewed the charter of the eight-year-old East India Company, an association of merchants and manufacturers, giving it a trade monopoly in Asia that was limited neither by time nor by space.

The British could not have chosen a more propitious time to appear on the scene. In the north the Mogul Empire, still rich and apparently entrenched, was actually already in decline, and the Hindu Marathas of western India were nibbling at its frontiers. The petty principalities girdling central India were seething with wars, plots and alliances. In the south, the great Hindu Vijayanagar Empire had fallen. India was in fact in ferment, and the early English traders were in an enviable position to exploit the situation.

From the opulence of its courts and temples, India appeared to be a market place which would attract any merchant. But the ostentatious wealth of maharajas and upper castes that dazzled the early Englishmen apparently was not reflected in the living standards of the Indian masses. Some accounts indicate that in earlier centuries India's per capita income may have been as high as that of any nation in Europe. But economic decline had paralleled the deterioration of the Mogul Empire.

Sharp-eyed Europeans who looked beyond the palace walls were not impressed. Noted François Bernier, a French physician at the Mogul court: "The inhabitants have less the appearance of moneyed men than those of many other parts of the globe." It is probable that the India of those times was marked by extremes of riches and poverty, much as it is today.

INDIA, in any case, was in no hurry to trade with the West. It has been deduced that early trade followed a pattern that was maddening to the tidy merchant princes of the East India Company. Western ships sold their cargoes in Indian ports, bought what spices, drugs and textiles they could, and sailed home as quickly as possible. Turnaround delays caused loss of interest and deterioration of ships and were a menace to the health of captains and crews. Indian traders soon perceived the need for haste and bargained accordingly, offering niggardly prices for English cargoes and demanding exorbitant charges for their own goods. To protect themselves from such commercial extortion, the harassed leaders of the East India Company sought permission from the Mogul court to establish agencies—"factories," as they were called—which could buy and sell goods and stockpile cargoes for the incoming ships. These factories—similar to those established by the Portuguese and Dutch, who came earlier—usually consisted of a few homes, offices and warehouses. The traders were permitted to maintain small contingents of troops to guard stores and furnish protection. This gave them a tiny suzerainty over Indian soil as well as a trading post. Thus were established the first enclaves of the European empires.

The late-arriving English fared badly in their first attempts to establish factories. It was not until 1613 that Emperor Jahangir allowed the East India Company to establish a trading center at Surat. But by the end of the century, the English traders had established important enclaves of commerce in Bombay, Madras and Calcutta, and a score of lesser ones elsewhere. Britain gradually began to overshadow its European rivals in India, and at the same time the once mighty Mogul Empire was visibly weakening in the continual wars with the Marathas. In 1687, the East India Company announced that it proposed to create such civil and military institutions "as may be the foundation of a large, well-grounded, sure English dominion in India for all time to come."

Events that were to enable the English to act on this proposal came to a head in the summer of 1756. The nawab of the Moslem state of Bengal, Siraj-ud-daula, a rash youth who had just mounted the throne, attacked the British fort at Calcutta. Most of the Europeans fled, but a group remained in the fort, which they soon surrendered. According to one witness, 146 of the captives were imprisoned in a guardroom that measured 18 feet by 14 feet 10 inches and had only two small windows.

THIS was the infamous Black Hole of Calcutta. It was June 20th—the stifling height of the Indian summer. The next morning, when the room was opened, only 23 of the prisoners were still alive. Some skeptical historians regard the Black Hole as a hoax, an atrocity story invented by the English. Certainly many of the details—the claim, for example, that the thirst-maddened survivors sucked perspiration from the sleeves of their suffocated comrades—are pure fancy.

Authentic or not, the Black Hole was sufficient provocation for rapid English action. An audacious young officer, Lt. Colonel Robert Clive, led a small British force against the nawab's legions and soon recaptured Calcutta. Siraj-ud-daula was compelled to grant more favorable terms for the East India Company's trade and to pay indemnification for the factories he had plundered. Clive, who had been packed off by his family to a clerkship in India at the age of 18, was a curious hybrid—part scoundrel, part genius. A confessed forger and briber, he nevertheless ranks with Cortés and Hannibal as one of the most daring military leaders in history. After his Indian victories he became the lion of London—a "Heaven-Born General," gushed William Pitt—and the most powerful man in India. Within a year after the nawab's defeat at Calcutta his subjects were conspiring against him—a conspiracy Clive willingly abetted. On June 23, 1757, with 800 British and 2,200 mercenary Indian troops, Clive launched a bold attack on the nawab's 50,000-man army at Plassey. Siraj-ud-daula's troops fought less than diligently, the English were victorious and the disreputable nawab was executed. Clive placed a puppet ruler on the Bengal throne and proceeded to enrich himself and his lieutenants by draining the princely treasury. From that time on, the British in India were not merely traders but conquerors.

During the next 60 years the East India Company established its sovereignty over most of the country. In some places the company gained power by bribery, in others by force. In some areas it governed directly, in others through puppet princelings. By 1820, British troops had wiped out resistance in the great Maratha Empire of western and central India, and the merchant adventurers had gained effective control of the subcontinent.

THE mission of the trader barons of the East India Company was economic aggrandizement. Clive and his comrades returned home millionaires, and for generations Englishmen after them went out to India and came home after a few years as rich as the Indian princes known as rajas. England overflowed with Indian money, and the East India Company paid annual dividends of as much as 200 per cent to its investors.

The traders had no wish to colonize and no notion of changing the Indian way of life. In the early years of the company's domain over India, local customs were solemnly observed: for good luck a coconut was broken at the beginning of each monsoon season, troops were paraded in homage to Hindu gods, and shops remained open on Sundays (not a holy day in India). Hindu and Moslem holy days were scrupulously observed. But among the many conquerors of India, the British alone remained aloof from the people. King Charles II, who reigned during the establishment of the British trading posts, was so unconcerned about India that when he received Bombay in the 1660s as part of the dowry of his Portuguese wife, Catherine of Braganza, he casually rented it to the East India Company for £10 a year.

THE separation grew over the years of the British raj (a word meaning "rule" which the British took over whole from Hindustani). In 1817, Sir Thomas Munro, later the governor of Madras, observed: "Foreign conquerors have treated the natives with violence and often with great cruelty, but none has treated them with so much scorn as we; none have stigmatized the whole people as unworthy of trust, as incapable of honesty, and as fit to be employed only where we cannot do without them. It seems to be not only ungenerous, but impolitic, to debase the character of a people fallen under our dominion."

While the East India Company governed India, the presence of troops guaranteed that rule, and the British Parliament took more and more of an active hand in Indian affairs. Customs which in British eyes were barbaric, but which were integral parts of the fabric of Indian life—including infanticide, ritual strangling and *suttee*—were outlawed or suppressed. British justice was introduced, and for the first time every Indian, from Brahmin to Untouchable, had his rights as an individual confirmed. But British rights were paramount, and despite the Kiplingesque nonsense of "the white man's burden"—that peculiar admixture of racial prejudice and proud conviction which held that it was the destiny of the white man to bring "lesser breeds" throughout the world the benefits of his material and spiritual achievements—India and its masses existed to serve and enrich Victorian England.

In its lust for income, the East India Company imposed land-revenue systems that disrupted the classic village economy of India. For centuries India had been a land of self-contained farms worked by hereditary landowners who each year paid tribute—anything from a sixth to a half of their harvests—to princely overlords. In some areas, the British created a new class of landlords called *zamindars* who, in return for proprietary rights to the land, turned over a fixed sum in taxes to the government each year. Elsewhere, peasants known as *ryots* were required to pay high rentals to the state in return for recognition of their ownership rights to the land they tilled. Defaulters were dispossessed, hereditary rights to the land were ignored. By the middle of the 19th Century, India was primed for trouble.

THE spark was struck in 1857, the year the British army planned the large-scale distribution of a new type of cartridge to the sepoys, the Indian troops serving in the British army. The shells were heavily greased and had to be bitten in order to expose the projectile. One day in the military camp near the town of Dumdum (where dumdum bullets were later to be manufactured), a low-caste Hindu asked a Brahmin soldier to lend him his *lota,* a brass drinking cup. Horrified, the Brahmin refused. According to Hindu caste strictures, he would have been defiled if he touched the cup after a low-caste had drunk from it. "You are very particular about your caste today," the low-caste is said to have shouted, "but you'll soon be biting cartridges that are made up of animal fat!" Few of the new cartridges had yet been issued, and those only on an experimental basis. The type of grease to be used had not been decided upon, and announcements to that effect were made. But words spread like a fever that all new cartridges would be greased with cow or pig fat. Both are forbidden to orthodox Hindus, and to touch pig fat is a sacrilege to Moslems.

What the Indians call the Great Revolt and 19th Century western historians called the Sepoy Mutiny began on February 26 when Hindu troops of the 19th Native Infantry, stationed at Berhampore, refused to accept the new cartridges. A month later, on March 29, troops of the 34th Infantry at Barrackpore attacked their English officers. By May 10, the revolt had spread to Meerut in northern India, where mutineers freed sepoys who had been jailed for refusing the cartridges. Marching on nearby Delhi, the Meerut mutineers captured the city easily and proclaimed the revival of the moribund Mogul Empire. The rebellion was confused, nearly leaderless and largely confined to northern and western India. After three months of siege, Delhi was recaptured by loyal sepoys and British troops who scaled the city's walls by placing ladders on the heaped bodies of their fallen comrades. Within two years the mutiny was suppressed. In England, it was agreed that the whole affair was the fault of the East India Company. In 1858, Britain transferred control of the government of India from the company to the British Crown.

FOR the next few decades India slumbered fitfully under the British raj. The country swarmed with English colonial officials, military men and fortune hunters. Yet there was still no confluence of the two cultures. "The best attitude, perhaps the only safe one, with Orientals, is that of complete superiority," said Sir John Lawrence, the pacifier of the Punjab.

More disastrous for their country, Indians think today, was the economic policy of the British government. England was in the midst of the Industrial Revolution, and as the British came to utilize India as a market for their cheap, factory-made goods, India's thriving handicraft industry inevitably declined and a whole class of artisans joined the ranks of the unemployed. At the same time the disintegration of the old farm economy accelerated. Increasing taxes hurt more and more of the small

CHRISTMAS IN INDIA

*Dim dawn behind the tamarisks—the sky is
  saffron-yellow—
As the women in the village grind the corn,
And the parrots seek the river-side, each calling
  to his fellow
That the Day, the staring Eastern Day, is born.
Oh the white dust on the highway! Oh the
  stenches in the byway!
Oh the clammy fog that hovers over earth!
And at Home they're making merry 'neath
  the white and scarlet berry—
What part have India's exiles in their
  mirth?*

*Full day behind the tamarisks—the sky is blue
  and staring—
As the cattle crawl afield beneath the yoke,
And they bear One o'er the field-path, who is
  past all hope or caring,
To the ghât below the curling wreaths of
  smoke.
Call on Rama, going slowly, as ye bear a
  brother lowly—
Call on Rama—he may hear, perhaps,
  your voice!
With our hymnbooks and our psalters we
  appeal to other altars,
And to-day we bid "good Christian men
  rejoice!"*

*Black night behind the tamarisks—the owls
  begin their chorus—
As the conches from the temple scream and
  bray.
With the fruitless years behind us, and the
  hopeless years before us,
Let us honour, O my brothers, Christmas Day!
Call a truce, then, to our labours—let us feast
  with friends and neighbours,
And be merry as the custom of our caste;
For, if "faint and forced the laughter," and
  if sadness follow after,
We are richer by one mocking Christmas
  past.*

SPIRIT OF EMPIRE was summed up by Rudyard Kipling in poems such as the one excerpted above. Born in India, Kipling traveled throughout the empire. The title of another of his poems, ''The White Man's Burden''—a phrase describing England's obligations to its newly won peoples—became a slogan of British imperialism.

farmers who concentrated on the production of basic food crops, ultimately causing them to lose their land. Meanwhile the large landholders saw their holdings increase as they devoted themselves to the production of such profitable commercial crops as cotton, jute and hemp. In the past the small farmers had managed to raise a sufficient surplus to help tide India over in famine years. But between 1800 and 1900 more than 32 million Indians died of starvation, 26 million of them in the last quarter of the century. Such disasters were inevitably blamed on the British.

It must be added, however, that British rule also brought many solid benefits to India. Under the British, Indians began to think of themselves as Indians in relation to the rest of the world, even though they thought of themselves as Bengalis or Kashmiris inside India. Political instability declined and the country settled down to a more orderly way of life. The railway network the British built was the largest in Asia; in addition they hacked roads out of jungles and deserts and irrigated large tracts of land. Modern medicine and sanitation methods were introduced, and India's mortality rate dropped sharply.

THE cause of Indian independence was unwittingly actuated in 1835 by Thomas Babington Macaulay, the eminent English scholar, poet and historian. His infamous ''Minute on Education'' was an arrogant condemnation of a civilized and cultured people. Its purpose, Macaulay explained, was to recommend English as a medium of higher education, in order to ''form a class who may be interpreters between us and the millions whom we govern; a class of persons, Indian in blood and color, but English in taste, in opinions, in morals and in intellect.'' Lord Macaulay envisioned this English-speaking group as a class of submissive political lackeys—clerks and interpreters who would faithfully carry out the orders of their British masters. Instead, English schooling and contact with western democratic ideas produced a class of intense nationalists who rediscovered their own culture and history, and who were the sires of the Indian revolution.

Nearly 500 new newspapers gave voice to Hindu nationalism in the late 19th Century and the early part of the 20th, but the advocates of freedom—strong men like the poet Rabindranath Tagore, the philosopher Mahadev Govind Ranade and the political strategist Bal Gangadhar Tilak—walked alone until, ironically, the Indian National Congress brought them together. Founded in 1885 by a Scotsman, the Congress was originally intended to promote Anglo-Indian understanding. Instead, it became a forum for nationalist ideas and a hotbed of conspiracy against the British raj.

The dynamic leader of the freedom movement was Tilak, a Brahmin and an instinctive politician. He wanted nothing less than complete independence for India. "*Swaraj* [freedom] is my birthright, and I will have it," was his slogan. Tilak preached violence and condoned assassination, and for his political activities he was sentenced to six years in prison.

A devout orthodox Hindu, Tilak was a stout defender of ancient customs, including child marriage. To cement the nationalist movement he freely relied on religion—Hindu India's most powerful unifying force. A scholarly man, Tilak invoked fiery slogans from the old holy books. "In the context of Indian politics," wrote the Indian politician and historian K. M. Panikkar, "the injunction, 'Therefore O, son of Kunti, arise and fight,' could have only one meaning, and Tilak drove the philosophy home with his agitational methods."

A BRILLIANT contemporary and an implacable foe of Tilak was Gopal Krishna Gokhale, the leader of the moderate wing of the Indian National Congress during the years of ferment around the turn of the century. The two men had much in common: both were Brahmins, both came from the state of Maharashtra and both were patriots who made heavy personal sacrifices for their beliefs. Both sought the same end—liberty—though they followed different means. Gokhale was a realist who practiced the art of the possible, while Tilak called on ancient gods and clamored for immediate freedom at any price, however bloody.

Inevitably the two clashed, and for years they fought for control of the Congress party. Once, after Tilak had tongue-lashed him for his policies of moving slowly and cooperating with the British, Gokhale turned on him bitterly. "Do you think, my friend," he asked, "that we are so devoid of self-respect and so base as to be happy at our country being under foreign yoke? I would have my country free today, if that be possible. But is it possible? Can we work on that basis? In politics you must consider what is practicable. We can in no way bind future generations. Who are we to bind them irrevocably? We are doing what we, in our time, consider best and practicable." The moderates withstood the challenge of the radicals until Gokhale's death in 1916.

THERE were other shadows on the horizon. The Hindu religious revival stimulated by the activities of Tilak and his fellow agitators widened the gulf between Moslems and Hindus. The Moslems, more fearful of a Hindu-dominated India than of a British-dominated one, began a separatist movement in the 1900s, which ended after World War II with the independence of Pakistan.

Throughout the period, Tilak and his followers had been agitating against the British. In Bengal, the Punjab and Maharashtra they instigated a reign of terror. But the British met terror with repression, and the net practical result of Tilak's campaign was exactly nothing. The Indian masses had no arms. The organized power of Britain was too great to be shaken by a few acts of violence. It remained for a British-educated preacher of nonviolence, one Mohandas Gandhi, the young lawyer who was fighting for the rights of Indians in South Africa while Tilak and Gokhale contended for power at home, to shake loose the mighty grasp of imperial Britain. In due course Gandhi would lead one seventh of the world's population to independence.

Troops drill and officials are conveyed by sedan chair and canopied cart at the East India Company's compound in Bombay in 1767.

The Blight and Blessing of British Rule

Britain's rule of India, which fanned out from the East India Company's early trading centers, combined commercial exploitation with political enlightenment. Cheap English factory-made products depressed India's handicraft industry and deprived millions of a livelihood. Maharajas ruling the myriad princely states grew richer as the British bought their allegiance, while high taxes impoverished the peasants, often forcing them from the land. But Anglo-Saxon codes of law, firmly established in India's judicial system, and concepts of individual rights, preached by the British and studied by Indian intellectuals, inspired India's growing nationalism. In time Britain's democratic traditions became the fabric of free India's constitution.

Below, a Bengali harbor full of clipper ships and a new East India garrison, Fort William, testify to British power in the 18th Century.

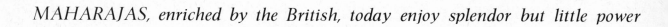
MAHARAJAS, *enriched by the British, today enjoy splendor but little power*

ORNATE SETTING of a grand palace reception hall (*opposite*) surrounds the wife of the Maharaja of Vizianagram.

STATELY PARADE for the marriage of the Maharaja of Jaipur's daughter includes courtiers and a jeweled elephant.

SURVIVING TIE with Britain underlies a warm welcome for a visiting monarch

LAWN PARTY in 1961 at the President's Palace in New Delhi unites Britain's Queen Elizabeth, India's President Rajendra Prasad, Vice President Sarvepalli Radhakrishnan (*left*) and Nehru's sister, Madame Pandit (*far right*). India, which owes the Queen no allegiance, gave her an exuberant reception as head of the Commonwealth.

HUMAN BLOCKADE is set up on a railroad by practitioners of *Satyagraha,* the doctrine of mass noncooperation worked out by Gandhi to topple the British raj.

5

Gandhi: Politician and Saint

HE was a strange little man: ugly, and at first glance almost comical in appearance. His enormous, pointed nose overshadowed a straggly mustache. His jutting ears were too large for his round, bald head. Cheap spectacles gave an owlish look to his bright, intelligent eyes. He always wore a *dhoti,* a garment that exposed his knobby knees and spindly shanks. He could carry all his worldly possessions in a kerchief, and to his humble, poverty-ridden countrymen he was a saint.

No such free and independent India as exists today could have been created but for the work of this wispy holy man. Before Mohandas Karamchand Gandhi became the adored Mahatma—the Great Soul—of modern India, the Indian National Congress was little more than a debating society of middle-class intellectuals agitating for the new notions of nationalism, sovereignty and emancipation which they had read about in western books. It was Gandhi, with his appeal to ancient religious precepts and his call for bold revolutionary tactics, who won the mass backing for the Congress party that was finally to overcome the most widely spread empire the world had ever known.

Gandhi was a prophet who struggled all his life to attain the Hindu ideal of truth. He insisted always that he was a religious leader, not a politician. "I am trying to introduce religion into politics," he often said. Yet he was a man of action as well as a man of the spirit, and it was the combination of these qualities, often manifested in most contradictory fashion, that made him one of the most powerful leaders of the 20th Century. It implies no disrespect to his saintliness to say that he was a foxy kind of saint. Unbending on matters of principle, he could move with the supplest flexibility when it came to matters of tactics. In the managing of men, his meekness concealed steel.

GANDHI was born in 1869 in a small northwestern state in which both his father and grandfather had served as prime minister. His strictly orthodox Hindu family belonged to the businessman subcaste, the Modh Bania; the name "Gandhi" means "grocer" in the Gujarati tongue. We know from his almost embarrassingly frank admissions that Gandhi had his share of ordinary human frailties and faults. As a boy he violated orthodox Hindu restrictions by eating goat's meat in secret and suffered a horrible nightmare in which a live goat kept bleating inside his stomach. In accordance with traditional Hindu custom he was married at 13, and he remained married to his faithful wife, Kasturbai, for 62 years. But he never got over his "shame" at his early "lustful love." His autobiography relates that at the moment of his father's death he and Kasturbai were in bed together—"a blot I have never been able to efface or forget." For three years he lived as a poor student in London, studying for a law degree while trying to keep a vow never to touch meat, wine or a woman. He bought a dress suit and liked ballroom dancing well enough to take violin lessons in an effort to improve his sense of rhythm.

Back in India, he made an indifferent start at the law. Then, in 1893, a chance came for him to go to South Africa to represent a Moslem firm in a damage suit. In South Africa the shy young barrister found himself. Appalled at the treatment of the Indians who had settled there, he started a long struggle against local legal and social discrimination.

As spokesman for the downtrodden Indians of Natal and the Transvaal, Gandhi scored many sharp points in the courts. But he also conceived and proposed a radically new line of resistance. The ancient Hindu rule of *ahimsa* (nonviolence) was, he said, the first law of life. He had read the essays of Count Leo Tolstoy, the Russian novelist and exponent of nonviolent resistance to evil authority, and the works of the British reformer John Ruskin, who preached the dignity of manual labor and urged a return to the simple life. The writings of the 19th Century American thinker Henry David Thoreau reinforced Gandhi's interest in the doctrine of deliberate disobedience to unjust power. These elements he combined into a belief of Christlike simplicity: oppose hate with love, greed with openhandedness, lust with self-control; harm no living creature.

Satyagraha was the name Gandhi gave to his program of mass nonviolent resistance. In literal Sanskrit the word means something like "steadfast grasping of truth"; Gandhi translated it freely as "soul force." He urged his followers to conquer by love. Gandhi himself was beaten, jailed, nearly lynched and repeatedly subjected to indignities. Yet, during the Boer War, in the midst of his struggles against the government, he raised and commanded an ambulance unit of Indians which served with distinction with the government's forces. Under the fascinated eyes of Indian newspaper readers back home, the Indian community of South Africa practiced soul force with such effect that by 1914 the government agreed to the removal of most of the injustices against which Gandhi had fought. In 1915 Gandhi returned to Bombay, preceded by a hero's reputation.

IN the first years after his return, Gandhi's activities were manifold. He toured the Indian countryside. He threw himself into a successful campaign to improve the lot of the miserable tenants of European planters in northern Bihar and that of the millworkers of Ahmedabad. He saluted all Untouchables as "children of God," invited a family of Untouchables to live with him and his followers, and later formally adopted their daughter. The gentle ascetic in a *dhoti* —eating like the poorest of the poor, proclaiming that manual labor is essential to the good life—won the hearts of millions. It was a season of restlessness in Indian life. During World War I, 1,401,350 Indian troops were mobilized and 43,695 died in action. Gandhi himself had helped the British recruit Indian troops. Expectations of greater freedom ran high. But British repressive measures, notably the Rowlatt Act, which continued the wartime suppression of freedom of speech, press and assembly, seemed in 1918 and 1919 to indicate that the government meant to go back on its wartime promise of "responsible government in India." Gandhi, convinced that the British would never willingly give India Dominion status, now came forward to oppose the raj. His proposal: *Satyagraha* for freedom.

BUT even before *Satyagraha* could get beyond the preliminary phase—a general suspension of economic activity—Gandhi's call for nonviolent opposition led to violence. Riots broke out in Delhi, Bombay and the Punjab. Filled with remorse at the spectacle of bloodshed, Gandhi asked all India to fast and pray with him for 24 hours to recover its discipline, proclaimed himself guilty of a "Himalayan miscalculation" and called off *Satyagraha*.

Gandhi announced his intention to fast on April 13, 1919. On that very day an event took place in the Punjab that decisively turned the course of Indian history. In defiance—or in ignorance—of a newly imposed governmental ban on public meetings, a crowd of 10,000 to 20,000 Indians had gathered in a garden in Amritsar. Arriving with a detachment of troops, Brigadier General Reginald Dyer, an Indian-born British officer of the old school, abruptly ordered his soldiers to fire into the crowd with the intention, he later declared, of producing "a sufficient moral effect." The firing continued

for 10 minutes. The grounds had only a few narrow exits. At least 379 persons were killed, and more than 1,140 were wounded.

Horrified and alarmed, Indians of all classes united against the British. They felt that their country's great efforts in the war had been betrayed. India's most famous poet, Sir Rabindranath Tagore, renounced his knighthood. Others also repudiated British honors. For Gandhi the Amritsar Massacre was decisive. It forced him to devote his full energies to politics. In their sense of helplessness before such a show of brute force, politically conscious Indians looked to Gandhi's revolutionary resistance program as their only possible hope. One of these was the young patrician Jawaharlal Nehru, who had joined the Indian National Congress shortly after his return from England. By his example young Nehru persuaded many westernized Indians to put aside their misgivings about Gandhi's homespun Hinduism.

Because of his growing popularity with the Indian masses, Gandhi overshadowed other Congress leaders at the 1919 session. A year later, the Congress adopted Gandhi's program of nonviolence and noncooperation in order to achieve self-government within—or without— the British Empire. Indian nationalism turned into a mass movement. "The British," wrote Gandhi, "want us to put the struggle on the plane of machine guns. . . . Our only assurance of beating them is to keep it on the plane where we have the weapons and they have not."

FOR the next quarter of a century the world was to witness the strangest confrontation in history. On the one side towered the mighty British Empire, personified by a panoplied viceroy. On the other, usually caricatured wearing a safety-pinned diaper, squatted the mild little Mahatma at his spinning wheel. It was not an entirely unequal confrontation: the little man had weapons—moral weapons— that could hurt. Uncomfortably the British tried to stand fast, while Gandhi beamed love at them, his sari-clad women followers lay down on railroad tracks and other *Satyagrahis* blocked pavements outside British shops. Often the protests would lead to shooting, but then Gandhi would call off the campaign and punish himself for his followers' transgressions by imposing another fast on himself.

In 1930, Gandhi, accompanied by 78 members of his *ashram*, or community of followers, staged a 24-day "salt march" to the sea in protest against the government's salt monopoly, stirring so many peasants to undertake saltmaking that the government arrested 60,000 of them, including Gandhi. But Gandhi jailed was as troublesome as Gandhi free. The government was paralyzed by growing rebellion. In the end, the British were forced to release Gandhi and other Congress leaders, and to hold a meeting with him. In England that distinguished devotee of empire, Winston Churchill, recoiled in horror at the "nauseating and humiliating spectacle of this one-time Inner Temple lawyer, now seditious fakir, striding half-naked up the steps of the Viceroy's palace, there to negotiate and to parley on equal terms with the representative of the King-Emperor." Yet the talks proceeded; and Britain for the first time found itself forced to talk to India—or to an Indian—as an equal. Another time, while imprisoned by the British, Gandhi started a fast to the death in protest against the government's decision to place India's 50 million Untouchables on a separate electoral roll; on the sixth day, as all India waited in hushed tension and the frail Gandhi's life ebbed away, the British approved a compromise that removed the threat of political distinctions between Untouchables and caste Hindus. "I always get my best bargains behind prison bars!" Gandhi once chuckled.

BASICALLY, Gandhi's hold on Indians was founded on his appeal to old Hindu ideals. There was a danger in this kind of strength that was not long in appearing. From the beginning, Moslems had been suspicious of Hindu influence in the Congress and the alleged ties of certain Congress leaders—not including Gandhi—to militant Hindu revivalist groups. When the Congress voted in 1920 to back Gandhi's nonviolence program, British-educated Mohammed Ali Jinnah, a Moslem and longtime Congress leader, walked out. Jinnah, a Bombay lawyer, was austere, westernized, brilliant and often arrogant. No fanatic nor even a particularly devout Moslem, he ate pork, drank, and was married to a non-Moslem. Jinnah became chief of the Moslem League, which had been founded in 1906 as a counterpoise to the Congress, and before long he was Gandhi's political rival. In 1928 the Congress party issued a blueprint outlining a centralized parliamentary government, and the absence of any concession in it to the Moslem League's demands for political safeguards seemed to confirm Jinnah's cry that India's 80 million Moslems would be outvoted and discriminated against by 250 million non-Moslems when the British left India. Jinnah called for a continuation of the system whereby Hindus and Moslems voted separately and for a federal form of government in which predominantly Moslem areas would be semiautonomous—a demand which Hindus said was inspired by British "divide and rule" strategy.

DURING the years before World War II, a profound change took place in Indian politics. Gandhi's work—and London's debate over the 1935 act which granted limited self-rule—disclosed that the British Empire was not after all immovable. Almost imperceptibly the Indians began to think not only of ridding themselves of the British but of the problem of controlling India after the British had departed. One result was the emergence of the Hindu-Moslem question to the forefront. In 1937, after Congress ministries had been elected to office in seven of British India's 11 provinces, the Moslem League promptly denounced all of them as Hindu dictatorships.

Within the Congress itself there were significant shifts. As the possibility and probability of independence neared, Gandhi moved toward the political sidelines. He devoted most of his energies to the plight of the masses, assisting the Untouchables, proposing improved sanitation and agricultural methods to farmers, drawing plans for village education. In the past he had sometimes given the impression that what kept India from being free was not the British but such trappings of modern civilization as the railways, factories, machine-made goods, medical science and modern jurisprudence, in addition to neglect of the cow. It still appeared in the 1930s that Gandhi's solution to India's economic problems was to return to the village economy of the past, an answer that was manifestly inadequate for an India approaching the middle of the 20th Century.

The most winning voice among Gandhi's lieutenants in the Congress party was that of the articulate and magnetic radical, Jawaharlal Nehru. Nehru was a high-caste Kashmiri Brahmin and as westernized as any Indian could become. His father, Motilal Nehru, one of India's richest and most brilliant lawyers, was a great admirer of British ways and British traditions. In the Nehrus' magnificent home in Allahabad, Jawaharlal and his sisters had been brought up in a cosmopolitan atmosphere, exposed to Islamic culture as well as English tutors, English conversation, and English books, ponies and dogs. With such a background, plus Harrow and Cambridge, Nehru was too British to be overly impressed by the British. He wanted freedom from both British imperialism and Hindu orthodoxy. Less concerned than Gandhi with the religious base of ethics, he was nevertheless an ardent supporter of the Mahatma, had gone to jail in an early civil-resistance campaign and was regarded by Gandhi as his spiritual son. It was apparent that he was also Gandhi's political heir.

WORLD WAR II brought the British to their last round in India. The Congress demanded immediate independence in 1939; when London refused, the Congress ordered its provincial ministers to resign their offices. Jinnah came out for the idea of an independent Pakistan. A British plan to transfer power to the Indians over all but military affairs broke

SOME GANDHI SAYINGS

"Love and exclusive possession can never go together. . . . The body is our last possession. So a man can only exercise perfect love and be completely dispossessed if he is prepared to embrace death and renounces his body for the sake of human service. But that is true in theory only. In actual life, we can hardly exercise perfect love, for the body as a possession will always remain with us. Man will ever remain imperfect, and it will always be his part to try to be perfect."

"The true source of rights is duty. If we all discharge our duties, rights will not be far to seek. . . . Action is duty; fruit is the right."

"Exploitation of the poor can be extinguished not by effecting the destruction of a few millionaires, but by removing the ignorance of the poor and teaching them to non-cooperate with their exploiters. That will convert the exploiters also. I have even suggested that ultimately it will lead to both being equal partners. Capital as such is not evil; it is its wrong use that is evil."

"Truth needs no publicity other than itself."

"Non-cooperation is not a movement of brag, bluster or bluff. It is a test of our sincerity. It requires solid and silent self-sacrifice. It challenges our honesty and our capacity for national work. It is a movement that aims at translating ideas into action. . . . A non-cooperationist strives to compel attention and to set an example not by his violence, but by his unobtrusive humility. He allows his solid action to speak for his creed. His strength lies in his reliance upon the correctness of his position. . . . Speech, especially when it is haughty, betrays want of confidence. . . . Humility therefore is the key to quick success."

down. Gandhi, Nehru and nationalist leaders were imprisoned in 1942 after Congress called again for immediate independence, and in London Prime Minister Winston Churchill publicly rumbled that he had not become the "King's First Minister in order to preside over the liquidation of the British Empire."

THEN Labour won the 1945 election in Britain, and Indian independence was suddenly in the air. Equally in the air was the question of whether Indians—Moslem and Hindu—could agree among themselves on a scheme for self-government. Jinnah was adamant for a separate Moslem state. While Nehru was forming an interim all-India government in August 1946, Jinnah proclaimed "Direct Action Day." In Calcutta 6,000 Hindus and Moslems were killed in five days' rioting. Early in 1947, Prime Minister Clement Attlee announced that Britain would quit India "by a date not later than June 1948." To arrange the transfer of power, Attlee named as India's last viceroy Rear Admiral Viscount Mountbatten, great-grandson of Queen Victoria. The Viceroy consulted both sides, and when he informed Nehru and other leaders of the Congress that the Moslem League would revolt rather than accept an "all-India" government, the Congress leaders reluctantly replied that a separate Pakistan was preferable to chaos. So it came about that India and Pakistan became independent and separate states on August 15, 1947.

To Gandhi, independence on such terms was a defeat. Long before, in South Africa, he had said that the "crucial test" would come over the uniting of Hindus and Moslems. Now the two communities were filled with hate. He characterized the partition variously as "a spiritual tragedy," "an inglorious end" to India's long fight, and a possible prelude to "military dictatorship." For the first time in Gandhi's life ordinary people began to attack him. The Hindus abused him for favoring the Moslems; Moslems condemned him for standing in the way of a separate Pakistan.

Partition removed almost a quarter of India's territory. It split both the Punjab in the northwest and Bengal in the east into two separate parts. Hindu-Moslem riots, or "communal disturbances" as the British called them, were an old story in India, but nothing in the past could compare with the hideous war of extermination that burst forth as the British pulled out. With partition, some eight million persons were uprooted, and their uprooting left a gory, two-way trail of murder and bestiality seldom paralleled in human history. The gutters of Calcutta were stained with Hindu and Moslem blood. In the western Punjab there was scarcely a town where Sikhs were not put to the knife, and in the eastern Punjab Moslems were murdered in every village. At the Lahore railway station, Moslems cut the throat of every Hindu. Near Jullundar station, blood-smeared Sikhs ran through halted trains beheading Moslem men, women and children. Thousands died; the number who were injured, raped or abducted has never been determined.

WHEN New Delhi celebrated the British withdrawal from India on August 15, Gandhi was in Calcutta, where he had gone in an effort to stop the massacres. Now almost 78, he saw his 32 years of labor for an India of brotherhood spurned, his teachings of nonviolence betrayed. But India's masses still adored the Mahatma; they gathered en masse to hear him speak. Although his teachings were rejected, the people considered him a saint. In the areas Gandhi visited, the fighting soon ceased. Yet the tides continued to run against him. Sometimes extremists started fights, and once a bomb was exploded at one of the prayer meetings he conducted in New Delhi.

On January 30, 1948, Gandhi was late as he walked across the grounds to start one of his prayer meetings. As the crowd surged around him, Gandhi touched his palms together in the traditional Hindu greeting. A young Hindu editor elbowed his way through the crowd, produced a small automatic pistol and fired three times. Gandhi murmured: *"Hai, Rama* [O, God]," and died.

School children hold up a picture showing stages in the life of Gandhi. Their textbooks refer to him as "Father of the Nation."

The Nation's Unsilenced Conscience

"As Gandhi said" is a common expression in India today. The government invokes his name to justify its policies and the opposition uses it to protest against the government. At times only the merest lip service is given to Gandhi's teachings. But whenever India's leaders defend the Untouchables, assist the villagers or resist the temptation to coerce an unruly people, it is Gandhi's voice they heed. More than revered, Gandhi remains the nation's prickly conscience.

ADORING DISCIPLES, two of Gandhi's relatives lean lovingly on his arm during a speechmaking tour. Although close to his own family, Gandhi lived amid a host of doting aides and apostles. During his last fast in 1948 (*opposite*), they kept a faithful vigil as the exhausted leader vainly protested Hindu maltreatment of Moslems.

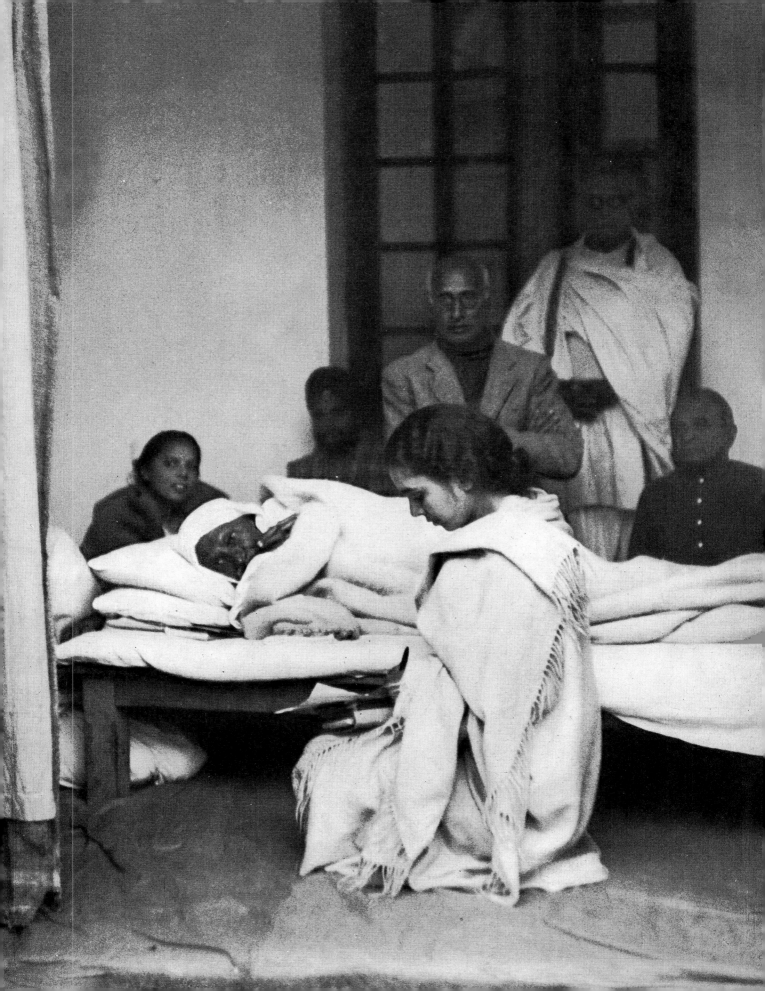

Wailing throngs watch as flames of a funeral pyre reduce Gandhi's body to ashes on the banks of the Jumna River early in 1948. Later,

in obedience to ancient Hindu custom, the Mahatma's ashes were immersed at the confluence of the Jumna and the Ganges Rivers.

6

Nehru: Consolidator of a Nation

AS the hour of India's independence drew near in 1947, the very survival of the new nation was in doubt. In the regions marked for partition between the new India and Pakistan, Hindus and Moslems were slaughtering each other by the thousands. In Delhi, tense crowds gathered. As the midnight hour struck in Parliament House, Jawaharlal Nehru, pale and handsome with a red rose stuck in his buttonhole, took the floor to speak on behalf of his country.

"Long years ago," he began, "we made a tryst with destiny, and now the time comes when we shall redeem our pledge, not wholly or in full measure but very substantially. . . . A moment comes, which comes but rarely in history, when we step out from the old to the new, when an age ends, and when the soul of a nation long suppressed finds utterance." At this fateful moment, when hideous massacres were rending India's body, Nehru summoned up the spirit of Gandhi. "The ambition of the greatest man of our generation has been to wipe every tear from every eye. That may be beyond us, but so long as there are tears and suffering, so long our work will not be over. This is no time for ill will or blaming others. We have to build the noble mansion of free India where all her children may dwell."

In the next months this lofty vision was almost blotted out by the bloody rioting between Hindus and Moslems. Order all but ceased to exist across the north of India and was threatened in Delhi itself. Nehru faced the challenge to authority with courage and resolution. And in the hour of crisis he even won the co-operation of his stalwart deputy prime minister, Vallabhbhai Patel. Strongly conservative, Patel had in the past opposed many of Nehru's theories and policies. A dedicated and tough-minded politician from Bombay, he too had been a trusted lieutenant of Gandhi. He was a much more skilled machine politician than Nehru ("Jawaharlal has an oratorical mind," Gandhi once said). The two men had often clashed and Gandhi had had to mediate and smooth over their differences. Now they stood shoulder to shoulder in the common peril.

Among Indians high and low, horror at Gandhi's killing created a revulsion against the extremists. Slowly the country righted itself, the resettlement of 8.9 million refugees from Pakistan was vigorously taken in hand, and in due course the world watched India proceed peacefully to stage the biggest democratic elections ever known. Nehru and the Congress party were triumphantly returned to power.

TODAY Nehru has held office uninterruptedly for a longer period than any other contemporary leader of a big democracy. But the experience of the violence attending India's birth has left its mark on Nehru's years of national leadership. It has turned Nehru into the consolidator of the nation more than the remaker of its society, and thus raised him above otherwise destructive political controversies.

Before independence, Nehru enjoyed a reputation as a militant revolutionary. He was impetuous, generous, devoted, widely read and well traveled in both East and West. Just as Gandhi mobilized the masses, Nehru drew the loyalty of the educated youth and middle class elements within the Congress party movement. He joined Gandhi's nonviolence campaigns,

but proclaimed himself an agnostic. His were the ideas of a new society—radical, humanitarian, egalitarian. It was Nehru who prodded the Congress party into declaring for outright independence, championed the cause of the impoverished peasants more ardently than any other Congress leader except Gandhi, and started the party on "economic planning" two decades before independence.

Neither then nor later was Nehru a doctrinaire Marxist, though many people accused him of it. But in those days he could say: "Socialism is a vital creed which I hold with all my head and heart." He also said: "Revolutionary changes cannot be brought about by reformist tactics. The reformer who is afraid of radical change or of overthrowing an oppressive regime and seeks merely to eliminate its abuses becomes in reality one of its defenders."

BUT Nehru in the prime minister's office found himself beset by problems that Nehru the idealistic revolutionary had never anticipated. The approach of independence had brought Nehru's brand of tolerant secular democracy face to face with intolerant militant Hinduism. After 1947 the prospect of imminent national catastrophe led him to adopt a more moderate course. Instead, he decided that India's revolution must proceed gradually and by mass consent, and to that end he directed that constitution-making should go right on through the worst of the communal rioting. Labeling communalism, localism and caste-mindedness the greatest menaces to a stable and united India, he sought to create the institutions and the climate of opinion that would weaken their influence.

Not to be confused with communism, communalism is the tendency of Indians to divide into religious blocs, i.e., Hindus against Moslems. To defeat communalism, Nehru demanded that the new state be secular, and he forced his colleagues to accept guarantees of rights for the country's 35.4 million Moslems. To offset localism, he ensured that the new central government's powers should be strong and that English should temporarily be retained as the *de facto* language used in the federal government, having equal status with Hindi. To strike at the worst feature of the caste system, he won a constitutional provision outlawing untouchability.

THE first big achievement of the new Indian state was the absorption of the 562 hitherto separate princely states. Before the British left, Lord Mountbatten, Britain's last viceroy, urged the princes to join either the new India or Pakistan. Patel, as Nehru's minister in charge of relations with these states, was entrusted with liquidating the principalities and merging them with the new nation. By a combination of force and persuasion Patel accomplished the job, giving the princes generous privy purses and letting them keep some of their extensive personal holdings.

Of these archaic states, the two biggest were the hardest to manage. The Nizam of Hyderabad, long familiar to Sunday supplement readers as "the richest man in the world," hoped to keep his large predominantly Hindu state (roughly equal in area to France) independent; then he toyed with the idea of joining Pakistan. Following a flurry of incidents, India imposed an economic blockade and after days of heated exchanges sent in troops. A year later the Nizam accepted Indian rule.

In the northwest, the Hindu Maharaja of Kashmir, panicked by an invasion of tough Pathan Moslem tribesmen from Pakistan, chose to join India, for although 77 per cent of his subjects were Moslems, the principal political movement in the state had close ties with Nehru and backed his secular policies. There followed a 14-month war in which the Indian army badly mauled both the Pathans and the Pakistani regulars sent in to back up the tribesmen. By the time the United Nations (brought in at India's request) achieved a cease-fire in 1949, India held two thirds of Kashmir. Since then, the U.N. has vainly tried to arrange a demilitarization of Kashmir as a prelude to a plebiscite, but India and Pakistan have been unable to agree on the terms for withdrawal of their forces. Actually the core of the dispute lies elsewhere: Kashmir is significant to the nationalists of both countries because its accession to Pakistan would appear to vindicate the religious basis on which that nation was founded. Nehru, who is a Kashmiri by descent, believes the security of India's Moslems depends on Kashmir's integration into a secular Indian state. He regards the case as closed, but India still holds Kashmir by force alone.

In the new India's political life, Nehru has also been consolidating his own dominant position. The death of Patel in 1950 removed the last strong figure within the Congress party leadership who might have opposed him. And when Nehru toured the country, huge crowds came to hear and adore him.

There was no spectacle on earth quite like these meetings between Nehru and the peasants. In his speeches to the humble country folk he made no attempt to preserve the polished style of his state addresses. These were long, extemporaneous talks, full of repetition and full of digressions about such things as drainage pipes and marriage ceremonies. Usually they were in Hindi, translated by impromptu interpreters in the crowd.

THESE contacts with the multitude, more emotional than verbal, provided what Indians call *darshan* (communion). The multitude was somehow reassured, not so much by Nehru's words as by his presence. In fact, he often lectured them like unruly children for clinging to cow worship or for trusting astrologers ("a business for stupid fools"), and the crowds invariably applauded. Nehru for his part seemed to lose every trace of fatigue and to become more alive, uninhibited and relaxed, evidently restored in spirit by the massed effulgence of a million shining faces. "The place where I function with the greatest ease," Nehru has said, "is before a large crowd. I find myself revitalized by the crowd."

Nehru's personal relationship to the multitude, however, is not always one of perfect understanding. During President Eisenhower's tumultuous welcome to Delhi in 1959, Nehru thought the people were pressing too close. Leaping from his seat in the official car, he climbed onto the jeep leading the procession and, waving his arms wildly, shouted to the crowds—in vain—to move aside. A popular story in New Delhi concerns a little girl who came home excitedly from a public ceremony and announced to her mother that Nehru had spoken to her. "What did he say, dear?" asked the mother. The little girl replied, "He said, 'Please get out of the way.'"

In the first country-wide elections in 1952, when no fewer than 105 million Indians went to the polls, Nehru and the Congress party won a substantial victory. The Hindu extremist parties were routed. The Socialists failed to do as well as expected, thereby suggesting that those who wanted moderate reform still hoped to get it from Nehru. It was the Communists who made the most surprising gains, winning successes in the south and returning enough members to Parliament—16 to Congress' 362—to qualify as an important opposition party. The result was to place in the forefront of Indian national affairs the immensely complex question of the transformation of society.

INDIA'S first five-year plan, launched in 1951, was an extremely cautious venture into the field of socialized planning, being little more than a glorified public works program. A series of good crop years, however, enabled the government to claim a 19 per cent rise in agricultural output under the program. Then late in 1954, when everybody was talking about China's big planned advances, Nehru returned from a visit to Peking and observed that India must move ahead faster. He announced that under the second five-year plan, to start in 1956, India would double its rate of public investment, give priority to heavy industry and drive for a 25 per cent higher national income.

Apart from the challenge of Communist competition in Ghina and in India, it was high time for India to make the strongest possible effort to expand its productivity. The 20th Century population explosion had detonated in half a million Indian villages, magnifying a problem already tremendous, and the number of mouths to feed was increasing at the rate of 10 million a year. The first five-year plan had managed to increase the average annual income of every Indian from $59.64 to $64.26. The second plan inched India's per capita income forward by another nine per cent. Iron and steel production more than doubled, the country began to make its own locomotives and heavy machinery, and enough dams were built and catch basins and wells dug to provide India with a significant increase in irrigated land.

IN 1961 Nehru launched India's third five-year plan, which is to cost $25 billion, or as much as the first two plans put together. Its goals are correspondingly ambitious: 70 per cent higher industrial output, 30 per cent more farm production (thereby making India self-sufficient in food), and a one third higher national income. By the time the plan has been completed, Indians hope to have raised the daily caloric rate of their 438 million people from 2,100 to an average of 2,300, or about 700 calories less than the U.S. rate. They expect to finance this huge program by raising taxes, by procuring funds from government-operated industries and from domestic savings, by increasing exports and by obtaining more than a billion dollars a year in loans and grants from abroad. The so-called "Aid to India Club"—those nations of the West which have consistently extended help to India (the U.S., Britain, Canada, France, West Germany) and also Japan and the World Bank—has offered a total of $2,286,000,000; the U.S. alone will make at least a billion dollars available. Russia has promised $500 million. Even with all this help India will be one billion dollars short, but it feels sure it can make up the difference.

By this succession of five-year plans, Nehru says he is taking India toward socialism. Yet socialism seems a long way off. Within the last decade the government has increased its legislative power to take over or to create industries of strategic or other special importance, and has nationalized both the country's largest commercial bank and the foreign and domestic life insurance companies. But that is the extent of the nationalization efforts, and in 1955 Nehru asked: "Why should public enterprise take over tasks that are being well performed by the private sector of the economy?" Under the third five-year plan, 64.4 per cent of all investment funds are to be allocated to the public sector. Yet today, after a decade of planned economy, private enterprise still accounts for 90 per cent of the country's gross national product.

Capitalism in India is indeed subject to regulation—though not so much, for example, as it is in the United States. The government taxes corporate profits and generally attempts to make business activities conform to government objectives. After independence the government began attempting to regulate foreign businesses operating in India, saying in effect: "You may operate here if you observe Indian laws, pay Indian taxes, use Indian labor and—when they are available—manufacture your goods from Indian materials." These regulations have since been eased. But Indian bureaucracy has not often made it easy for private foreign businesses to open new factories under these ground rules. Relatively few foreign enterprisers have had the patience and stamina and good nature to wade through the jungle of governmental red tape, round up all the countless licenses that are required, and sit through the interminable interviews that for years seemed to be part of the course. In India's first 11 years, foreign firms invested only $674 million in the country.

TODAY in India the past continues to be more visible than the future. Millions are homeless—living, sleeping and dying on the sidewalks of Calcutta and other cities. Some 67 million cattle roam the land unchecked, devouring food that could help sustain India's estimated nine million unemployed.

Yet in 10 years' time there have been undeniable gains. Many of the barefoot are shod, many who walked now ride bicycles, and millions have homes and eat better. Part of the gains in food production under the first five-year plan were ineffective because people simply could not buy what they needed, but now many Indians have at least a little money to spend. The country is forging ahead in atomic energy development, raising its steel capacity and rushing to completion a vast network of hydroelectric projects. More than 44 million Indians now attend school and college, and the number is to go up by a third in five years. The number of doctors, hospitals and universities is much larger than it was a decade ago.

AS India has bent to the task of creating a modern economy, Nehru has supervised the shaping of its political institutions from ever loftier heights. In 1950 India formally became a republic, though it remained within the British Commonwealth. Then agitation increased in favor of reorganizing the nation into new states conforming more or less with linguistic areas. Many thoughtful Indians felt that Nehru was slow to come to grips with this potentially dangerous problem. But in 1953 riots among the Telugu-speaking people of Madras pushed the Prime Minister into announcing the creation of Andhra, the first Indian state to be created along linguistic lines, and soon thereafter he promulgated a plan reorganizing all India into 16 such states and six union territories.

A rash of resignations, demonstrations and riots broke out. In Bombay state, one of the newly created units, scores died in the worst fighting since partition. Nehru came down from his Olympian eminence and, with characteristic impetuosity and heedlessness of personal danger, rushed to Bombay. "Who lives if India dies, and who dies if India lives?" he cried in an impassioned speech that moved many Congress leaders to tears. Then he acted to divide Bombay in two, one for the Marathi-speaking people and one for the Gujerati-speakers.

The question of language and disruptive local loyalties in India is still unresolved. Discussing the seriousness of this matter for India's future, some intelligent Indians argue that to bind all their countrymen into one nation it may yet be necessary to teach three languages in every school in the country—English (the language bequeathed by the educators of the present ruling generation), Hindi (the language of about 40 per cent of all Indians) and the appropriate local tongue.

AMONG Indian voters, however, the combination of Nehru's magic name and the Congress party's big machine has carried the government to repeated victories at national and local levels. Other national parties have made no significant headway. The Communists actually won control of the southern state of Kerala in the 1957 elections, but they bungled badly while in office, antagonizing a powerful local caste and even committing the enormity of firing on striking workers. After less than a year Delhi was called upon to remove the Red rulers and, under the constitution, established federal rule in Kerala.

Thus Nehru stands today, the biggest man in India, not effectively challenged either by right or by left. He is prime minister, foreign minister, chief of the atomic energy program and chairman of the country's planning commission. He has also held the posts of defense minister, finance minister and president of the Congress party when he felt these offices particularly needed his personal attention. At home as abroad, his policy has been to steer a central course between main forces. This has turned the man who once was the British Empire's foremost revolutionary into a nation builder, the leader of all his people. To play his new role, Nehru has had to slow the pace, let issues slide and forgo radical initiatives of a more controversial character.

An old admirer who is currently in the opposition has characterized Nehru as "explosive in speech, disciplined in action, impulsive in gestures, deliberate in judgment, revolutionary in aim, conservative in loyalty, reckless of personal safety, cautious about matters affecting Indian welfare." He adds that Nehru is "at once personal and detached, human and aloof, with the result that he appears now fond, now cold, now proud, now modern. He is an aristocrat in love with the masses, a nationalist who represents the culture of the foreigner, an intellectual caught up in the turmoil of an emotional upheaval—the very paradox of his personality has surrounded it with a 'halo.' "

Power has made Nehru more irritable but less impatient: he is more amenable to compromise, not so much with the politicians as with the people. He is still the agnostic ready to berate his vast audiences for devotion to holy days, holy cows and fraudulent holy men; but he never does much about these popular institutions and traditions. Though he may rail at India's masses for their ingrained habits of inefficiency, tardiness and cheerful anarchy, he has the same affection for them that they have for him, and this is the wellspring of his strength.

SO it is that Nehru monopolizes all leadership; and the Congress party monopolizes all offices. Inevitably, the party of the revolution has gradually lost its crusading zeal, grown corrupt and concerned itself with little but position and patronage. Sensing the loss of impetus, Nehru pronounced himself "flat and stale" a few years ago, and made as if to step down. The party politicians would not hear of it. Not too displeased, Nehru stayed on and was confirmed in his feeling of the indispensability of his leadership.

Yet even those Indians who feel that the leadership of the nation may be flagging agree that a start has been made. Nehru's India is a country with majority rule, parliamentary institutions and a free press. It is unlikely that anyone will be found who can precisely fill Nehru's shoes, but when Nehru goes and ordinary politics start up, the essential national unity and democratic institutions will be found ready. Indeed, this unity and the very fact that the necessary institutions of the new India do exist may prove to be the final monument to Jawaharlal Nehru.

Nehru (second from right) and the Indian Planning Commission meet to draw up the intricate schedules for a five-year plan.

A Dominant Party's Pragmatic Regime

The Congress party, which led the fight for independence, runs the government of India. Party members control the ministries, the Parliament and the vital Planning Commission. But though the Congress party is supreme, its ranks are sharply divided between right and left wings, held together by Nehru's strong personality. Some observers feel such a division is a force for democratic flexibility as the one dominant party works to modernize the nation.

but remains outside Nehru's government

JOINED BY VILLAGERS, frail Vinoba Bhave takes one of his arduous walking tours through India (*left*) to find people who will donate land to the landless. His mushrooming *bhoodan yagna* (land-gift sacrifice) movement, begun in 1951, has collected more than four million acres of land, which is being given to needy villagers.

RIGHT-WING CORE, Agriculture Minister S. K. Patil (*above*) and Finance Minister Morarji Desai (*below*) are strong conservative forces within the Congress party.

PARTY POWER, former Congress President Indira Gandhi (*left*) is Nehru's influential daughter.

NEHRU'S INTIMATE, Minister of Defense Krishna Menon is outspoken, unpopular and anti-U.S.

STAFF QUARTER, the Secretariat (*left*) forms part of the core of Chandigarh, the Punjab's striking new capital designed by France's master architect Le Corbusier.

HIGH COURT, Chandigarh's tribunal (*opposite*) has honeycomb walls to defy the Punjabi heat. The city will have residential areas that override caste distinctions.

7

Unchanging Round of Village Life

HIS name may be Abdul, Ram, Ranjit or Gopalaswami. The chances are four to one that he is illiterate, and he is often ill-fed. He is frequently in debt to a moneylender, and even if all goes well he still lives on the brink of starvation; illness, drought and crop failure constantly plague him. He typifies eight out of every 10 Indians, and for centuries he has gone his way silent and unchanging while emperors and kings and conquerors have strutted and plundered and disappeared. He is the Indian villager.

More than half of all Indian investments, public and private, have gone into industrial development in recent years. Yet though many five-year planners would rather discuss such impressive river valley development projects as Bhakra-Nangal in the Punjab, and the new million-ton-capacity steel plants, everybody at every level is aware that the economic salvation of India ultimately depends on the welfare and productiveness of the lowly village farmer. There are some 550,000 villages in India, and not only do farm workers make up 70 per cent of the population, but agricultural and allied activities account for nearly half of India's national income. With the population growing faster than statisticians had calculated (it is expected to reach 480 million by 1966), all authorities agree that the rate of food production must be vastly increased. Currently, Indian plans call for an increase from the present 76 million tons of food grains produced each year to an annual 100 tons. A team of American agricultural experts sent out by the Ford Foundation has estimated that if food production increases no faster than at present, India will be about 25 per cent short of meeting its bedrock nutritional requirements by 1966. "No conceivable program of imports or rationing can meet a crisis of this magnitude," the experts warn.

NOR does a way out of the food crisis appear to lie in the restriction of India's population explosion. Scattered around the country, there are some 1,800 government-maintained "family planning centers," where both men and women are given contraceptives and information on fertility cycles. Sterilization of both sexes is officially endorsed, and when an applicant is approved by state-appointed social workers or clinic doctors—he must already have at least three children, among other requirements—the government pays for the operation. Since 1956 more than 120,000 men and women have availed themselves of the privilege. Yet such figures are meaningless when measured against the Niagara of Indian births; each year the country adds the equivalent of the population of New York City to its numbers.

To deal more realistically with the food crisis, India in the years since independence has promulgated an impressive series of land reform laws and development programs to stir the village farmer out of his lethargy, improve his health and well-being, broaden his opportunities and induce him to change his ancient ways. Some of the programs have been outstandingly effective, others only partially so.

The legislation which broke up the vast hereditary holdings of the *zamindars* and other large landowners was, for example, excellent in intent, and it has had a profound political effect, bolstering popular confidence in the Nehru government as a democratic regime dedicated to the interests of the underprivileged. But the economic effects of the law have been widely debated. The breakup of the big holdings created not only the obvious problem of which farmers should receive redistributed land, but also problems of protecting farmers against eviction, of setting fair rentals and of assisting tenants to become owners. Land has been distributed in some areas, but in others the government has been reluctant to turn it over; the peasant has merely acquired a new landlord—the state itself. A deputy minister of the government says privately: "Congress will never give up that land because it is too valuable politically. They've got the peasants just where the *zamindars* had them—under their thumbs—and the land can be used to get votes."

Moreover, all too often the only accomplishment has been the fragmentation of large economic holdings into small, uneconomic ones. No one knows precisely how much land has been redistributed to the peasants; the official text of the government's present five-year plan notes: "As much of the legislation is quite recent, exact information regarding the extent to which ownership rights have been conferred on tenants is not available."

THE root of the problem, however, lies in the methods and poverty of the Indian farmer. It is of course hardly surprising that, like many peasant farmers elsewhere, he is largely unacquainted with modern agricultural methods and implements. But his attachment to traditional techniques, and the shortage of water in most parts of India, combine to make him the poorest farmer in the world. Non-irrigated land is at the mercy of the monsoon, which fails to deliver rain an average of two years out of every five. Where irrigation is available, the farmer cannot make use of it without making a considerable investment in equipment, an outlay beyond his means. In some villages, efforts to promote cottage industries such as hand weaving, spinning or the making of toys or furniture have been highly successful and give farmers a source of income. But these industries do not supply the farmer with large amounts of capital, and many villages lack knowledge of such opportunities to earn money. Chemical fertilizers, moreover, are not yet easily available to the farmer, and in many areas animal fertilizers are burned for cooking and heating because no other source of fuel is available. The Japanese farmer produces three times as much rice per acre as the Indian, and the Chinese twice as much.

The Indian farmer, in addition, makes little use of the traditional methods by which small farmers in other parts of the world increase their meager cash earnings. If he is a caste Hindu, there is no possibility of his engaging in the fattening of cattle, sheep and pigs for slaughter—and India, with no market for them, has more cattle (220 million head) than any other nation in the world. If the farmer is a strict vegetarian—and a high percentage of all Indians are—he will not keep chickens because he believes he must not eat them or their eggs.

Millions of Indian farmers live chiefly on the cereals and vegetables which they themselves grow, and any small surplus they may achieve is generally converted into cash. If the farmer keeps a cow, the butter often goes to a moneylender to help repay old debts, and the farmer and his family subsist on buttermilk. Malnutrition for most Indians thus begins with weaning and lasts through life. In many parts of India the farmer's diet is supplemented only by a cheap cooking oil which supplies a meager ration of fat. In vast areas, vegetables are not grown at all by villagers and fruit is available only at certain seasons. In some villages the poor Untouchables are the best nourished of all because they will eat anything.

THAT an enormous proportion of the population dies early is a known fact. Considerable efforts are being made to improve the health of the villagers. One of the most notable has been the campaign to stamp out malaria. Before the program started in 1953, an estimated 57 million persons in India contracted malaria—and about a million died of it— each year. Under the direction of public health technicians, villagers have drained swamps in malarial districts and spread DDT supplied through U.S. and World Health Organization funds. The number of fatalities has dropped to about 200,000 a year.

IT was to attack the basic causes of village poverty that India launched its Community Development program on October 2, 1952, the anniversary of Gandhi's birth. Begun on a comparatively modest scale and supported in part by American funds, the program has grown so rapidly that by October 1963 it will cover the whole country. Under the program, villages are grouped into "development blocks" of roughly 100 each. The program includes the building of roads, the improvement of sanitation, the reclamation of unused lands, the introduction of improved farming methods and the demonstration of new techniques. After training, the villagers are encouraged to help themselves—to build irrigation ditches, schools and clinics, and to improve local sanitation procedures. They are also encouraged to suggest projects to the government's technicians. Each unit has specialists in health, education, agriculture and other fields.

One of the theories embodied in the Community Development program is that villagers can be shown improvements that have been made in other villages and then be persuaded to duplicate them in their own. Often the theory works, but often it does not. Farm technicians generally agree that when a villager is taken in tow and shown that a steel plow will dig a deeper furrow than a wooden one, that planting good seeds will produce better crops and that digging a drainage ditch will benefit him and his family, he is willing, sometimes even eager, to give it a try. But the apathy of centuries is not easy to overcome. "The villager has not changed overnight his attitude toward officialdom," says an official 1960 publication of the Government of India.

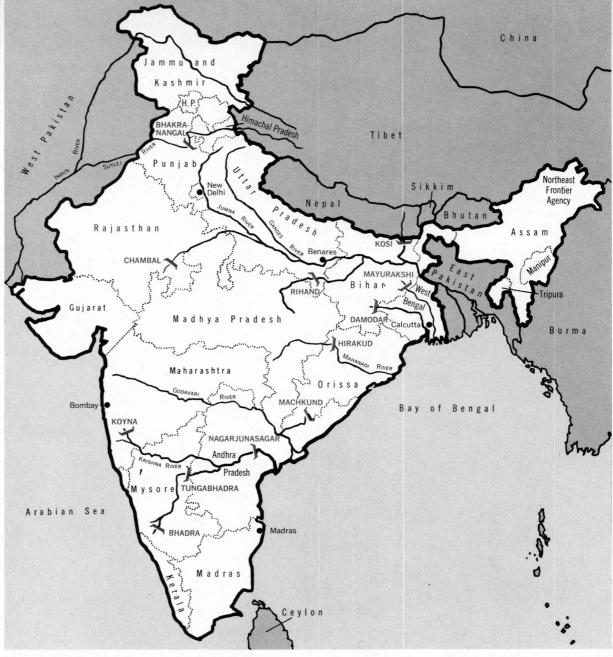

BOOST TO THE VILLAGES, 10 major river valley projects —shown by symbols on the map above—have already helped bring electricity for the first time to 11,000 communities and put 10 million new acres under irrigation. Being built under India's five-year plans, the projects also provide flood control and power for industry.

"He will still chuckle when something goes wrong with the demonstration plots; he is inclined to take refuge in his massive rustic obstinacy from the efforts of the young, earnest and enthusiastic village level workers to persuade him to depart from ancestral customs." Yet the program has scored some notable successes. In the years since its inception, life expectancy has increased from 32 to 42 years, literacy (*Chapter 9*) has risen some 7 per cent and agricultural productivity 33 per cent.

In many a village, of course, life still goes on in the old ways. Consider one which we shall call Indpore. It is not a "typical" village because India has none. Indpore is a mythical community, which permits generalities. It is a small village with 160 mud houses, and it is unusually prosperous because its 439 acres lie on a flat and reasonably fertile plain. Indpore also is fortunate because, unlike many Indian villages, it is not completely dependent on the rains brought by the monsoon.

Indpore's 40-odd wells provide more than enough water to irrigate most crops, and in the dry season teams of men drive bullocks around the wells, providing power to lift 20-gallon buckets of water. Boys pour the water into the channels which lead into the squared fields.

NO one knows exactly how many people live in Indpore, and no one in the village is concerned about the exact count. For the unit of population in India is the "joint family." Such a family consists of a man, his wife, his sons, his unmarried daughters and his sons' wives and children. Often there are three or even four generations under one roof. The ruler of the family generally is the oldest male, and the rules of protocol demand that he be treated with great deference and respect. A sort of communism prevails in the joint family. All members of the household turn over their earnings to the head of the family and the money goes into a common pool. The joint family is an integral and important part of Indian life. It is an institution which provides basic security in Indpore and, indeed, throughout the country. "The warmth of belonging," remarks the French journalist Taya Zinkin in her book *India Changes!* "follows the Indian throughout the whole of his life, for he belongs not only within his immediate family but also within his extended family. . . . The family may quarrel . . . but the family is there to protect the child, the adolescent and the old against the hazards of fortune and the hostility of the outside world, for all are interdependent."

There are 160 families in Indpore; the largest single occupation group is farmers with 120 families. As in all villages various castes live apart from each other, and the 13 families of Harijans—Untouchables—live in a segregated area of crumbling mud huts and rude lean-tos. Every caste is represented in Indpore and there also are five families of Moslems. The Hindus are further split into 22 subcastes. The high-caste Brahmins own the bulk of the land, are rigidly orthodox and take the lead in seeing that all of Hinduism's rituals and ceremonies are observed. In fact, until the Brahmins were forced to sell most of their land to the government under a land reform bill, all of Indpore belonged to four of these high-caste families. And because the reform bill permitted each male member of a Brahmin family to retain 30 acres of land, the Brahmins remain the largest landowners in Indpore.

Ram Das is one of the villagers of Indpore. He is a small, emaciated, almost toothless little man of 42, whose habitual costume is a *dhoti.* Sometimes Ram also wears a short jacket of homespun cloth, and on very special occasions he dons a cinnamon-colored turban. Ram is illiterate, and he was a poverty-stricken tenant farmer until he received four acres of land when redistribution took place in Indpore. Ram had been working in the fields as far back as he can recall, and his father, grandfather and his grandfather before him, so far as he knows, also were tenants.

AT 42, Ram considers himself an old man; he looks it, and he feels it acutely because for the last two years he has been coughing and having occasional hemorrhages. The first time he had a hemorrhage Ram was so frightened that he took some of the family funds—two rupees, the equivalent of 42 cents—and went to a village doctor. The doctor rubbed his chest with a large red stone which he said was a ruby, touched various other parts of his body with semiprecious stones and told Ram to drink a potion he gave him and the bleeding would stop. It never did, but Ram has not been back to the doctor because he hates to part with two more rupees.

Ram has less energy every season, and sometimes he cannot work at all, but he prays often and devoutly and he hopes eventually he will drive out the devil that is making him ill. For he knows that illness is caused by evil. Ram had an infant daughter who was stricken with smallpox, and he and his wife, Deepali, were so frightened of the powerful devil that had entered their home that they considered taking the child into the fields and leaving her there. They did not, but when the child died Deepali and Ram not only said the usual prayers for the dead after her cremation, but paid a Brahmin to sprinkle the interior of their home with milk, a custom associated with the universal veneration for the cow.

DEEPALI and Ram have had seven children altogether, but only three are still alive—two sons, 17 and 21, and a daughter, 11. Both of Ram's sons are married and they have five children between them, but Ram is becoming increasingly worried because he has not yet married off his daughter. For the last two years he has hoped to earn enough from his crops to pay for her dowry, and perhaps even earn a little toward her wedding feast. But he has not saved enough yet. If Ram does not make it this year he is resolved to go to the *bania*, the moneylender. Secretly, Ram is afraid the *bania* might not let him have very much money, because for a dowry a man is supposed to spend more money than he can afford, and the cost of wedding feasts is increasing all the time.

Ram already owes the *bania* so much that for years he has been able to pay nothing more than the interest. Ram inherited part of the debt from his father, and though he has heard that a law has been passed which says that he does not have to recognize this debt, Ram feels it is his duty to pay it. As far as Ram is concerned, the law is worthless—like the law which says that a girl may not marry until 15. Ram believes the best age is nine or 10, though he does not believe a girl should live with her husband until she reaches puberty.

Ram already has spoken about his daughter to the *gataka*, the marriage broker. He was told that he need only send along his daughter's horoscope and the *gataka* would find a young man of the same subcaste whose horoscope is harmonious. He plans to send the horoscope after he has accumulated a little more money toward her dowry and wedding feast.

Ram and his family live in a mud house with a small and rickety veranda. There are three small rooms in the house, and these are almost dark even at midday because the house has only one small window and one door. The door opens into a small courtyard where Ram keeps his two bullocks and an old cow which he addresses respectfully as "Mother." Except for a couple of shelves, a built-in mud stove, and several *charpoys* (string beds), there are no furnishings in the house. One of Ram's daughters-in-law has a lithograph of Lord Krishna hanging on the wall of the room she shares with her husband, and there is a small shrine festooned with tinsel garlands in the room Ram shares with Deepali. The shrine encloses a small image of Indra, the thousand-eyed god of the firmament who is Ram's family deity, and Deepali washes the image each day and places a token offering of food before it.

Deepali is the same age as Ram, a worn-faced wiry little woman with a gold nose ring. She is even more pious and old-fashioned than Ram. In accord with joint family custom, she berates her two daughters-in-law incessantly, and they slip around like frightened cats. Deepali will not allow her daughters-in-law to speak to their husbands in the presence of other members of the family. They do the cooking under her supervision. The family lives mostly on *chapattis* (unleavened wheat cakes) and *dal* (lentil soup), with occasional curried vegetables. The grandchildren are given watery buttermilk. Ram is always served first, his sons eat next; then Deepali has her meal with her daughter. What is left goes to the daughters-in-law and their children.

RAM invariably awakens before daybreak. After yawning loudly and noisily clearing his throat, he begins to recite prayers to Indra in a loud voice. As soon as he is satisfied everyone else is awake, he arises, always remembering to look at and touch a small gold ring which belonged to his father. He considers the ring a good-luck charm, and luck is necessary to ensure a successful day. Next he walks across the courtyard to the cowshed, touches his cow and raises his hand to his forehead in a sign of respect for Krishna, lord of herdsmen. He usually remains standing there to say the rest of his morning prayers.

Just before sunup he walks to the village pond for his morning bath. On the way he chooses a green twig to use as a toothbrush, though brushing his few loose teeth has by now become little more than a ritual. The stick with which he brushes his teeth should be 10 inches long, an inch shorter than one used by members of the Kshatriya caste, and two inches shorter than one used by a Brahmin, and so Ram is careful to see that it is not too long—although he does not quibble if it is shorter than necessary. After this ritual, he enters the pond wearing his *dhoti* and washes, while again chanting prayers. Ram bathes at least three times a day, as do many orthodox Hindus. Most Indians bathe at least once a day, and they would be perhaps the world's cleanest people if they had the proper facilities and enough changes of clothing.

AFTER his bath Ram returns to his home, usually with his sons, who by this time have joined him. The women of the household have had their baths at a nearby well, and after another short prayer before Indra, Ram has his breakfast. He always goes to the fields with his sons, but—except during the harvest season—he usually remains only long enough to give a few orders. On his way home he stops outside the house of the *sarpanch,* or headman, to listen to the eight o'clock newscast in Hindustani.

The *sarpanch* always has his radio on his front veranda, blaring forth at full volume. He presides over the *panchayat* (the village ruling body). The *panchayat* is an institution that goes back to ancient times; the word means an assembly of five, but in Indpore the *panchayat* has seven members, and the number varies from village to village. In modern India more than half of the *panchayats* are elected, and in some villages electioneering for the posts is as noisy and furious as it is in most municipal campaigns. In other villages, where the new electoral procedures have not yet been put in effect, elders gradually accede to their places in the *panchayat* because of rank or respect. In many villages the *panchayats* today serve as the major link between rural people and the government.

Ram is uneducated, and his only minor vice is that he frequently drinks too much country spirits during *Holi,* the spring festival. Still, everybody misbehaves somewhat during *Holi;* the lower classes parade around Indpore singing raucous songs and spraying other villagers with colored water. Ram's only other extravagance will be the marriage feast he gives for his daughter. He does not see himself as helpless and backward, and since he has acquired land of his own he proudly thinks of himself as a success. His basic philosophy is that the old ways are best and should not be changed, and that is true of caste, marriage or almost anything else. Although he has dutifully cast his ballot for the Congress party in the two national elections, he really is not concerned or much aware of his national government. Like other villagers since time immemorial he thinks of the government as something apart from him; if it changes, this will merely be the result of the good fortune or bad fortune of his masters.

OUT of the $15 or $20 cash he nets from his crops each year, Ram has hoarded a few rupees, which he keeps hidden away in a tin box. A portion of the money, he knows, will be used by his heirs to buy some pots of the clear butter known as *ghee* and, perhaps, some herbs and slivers of sandalwood to sprinkle on his funeral pyre. He is happy that he has a son to light the fire, and except for getting his daughter married, he cannot think of a thing he would like to do except make a pilgrimage to the holy city of Benares to bathe in the sacred river Ganges and store up a little merit for the next life.

Lasting Beauty in the Toil of the Hand

It is characteristic of Indian life that the human hand has been vested with an almost mystical meaning. The gesture is more eloquent than language in Hindu rites. In the country's dances the graceful swaying of the arms is a highly expressive movement. For in the Indian villages, now as centuries ago, the earth is tilled, its deep waters drawn and most produce made by the hand itself. A sustained campaign is being waged to overcome the villager's primitive methods, but his ways—embedded in tradition—are often hard to change. In his deliberate movements there is drudgery, but also poise and dignity. His handicrafts—which the government is encouraging as an economic asset to the villagers—give grace and pattern to a parched countryside. The Indian touch, however arduous, is one of timeless beauty.

RELAYING BUCKETS, women form a line (*opposite*) on a dam in Andhra Pradesh to draw water from the lake.

Colorful fabrics, woven by machine but dyed and printed by hand, glow on a flooring of cloth and earth as workers in Ahmedabad

put their goods out to dry in the sun. The production of cotton textiles has doubled since 1951 under India's Five Year programs.

EXUBERANCE *characterizes the Indians at outdoor play*

HARVEST FAIR in the village of Bharatpur (*opposite*) delights villagers who ride a hand-turned Ferris wheel. The fair also offers camel races, wrestling and dancing.

SPIRITED GAME of *hututu* —a favorite in India—engages youths in Bombay. One player tries to tag another but is out if he does not keep crying *"Hututu."*

At a market in Jaipur, beside a gateway in the city's ornate crenelated wall, a crowd mills around a pottery stand as birds and a calf

8

The Quickening Urban Pace

hunt for food. The old Nahargarh, or Tiger Fort, rises behind.

FRENETIC, crowded and shrill, the cities of India have an air of adolescence. For millenniums, the villages of the land have been the focus of national life, moving in plodding ancient ways, their pace equivalent to that of the bullocks who provide their major source of power. The cities are young. New Delhi, the nation's capital, was not even laid out until 1911. Greater Calcutta, the largest city in the country with a population of 5.5 million today, had only some two million persons within its environs just a generation ago.

"The city air makes a man free," ran a medieval European saying, and it is in the cities that 20th Century India is casting off the shackles of the past. In them reside the politicians, the administrators, the professionals and the businessmen whose plans and actions are shaping the India of the future. Until recently these men did not focus their constructive efforts on the cities. Instead, they turned their attention in the first years after independence to the towns and villages of the hinterlands.

India is a country basically agricultural in character. Enormous areas of it are perennially overrun by damaging floods but are still dependent for their water on the mighty, torrential rivers. Still other vast and semiarid tracts depend on the annual monsoon rains. When British India was partitioned in 1947, almost a third of the subcontinent's irrigated lands went to Pakistan. It was apparent to the planners of the new India that flood control and irrigation would have to take top priority. Almost half of the government's $4.9 billion investment in the first five-year plan, which was launched in 1951, was expended on irrigation and power projects and on measures directed toward the expansion of agricultural productivity. River valley development projects, some of them originally planned by the British but based to a large extent on the U.S.'s Tennessee Valley Authority, are being hastened to completion.

THE largest and most renowned, Bhakra Nangal in the Punjab, will bring 10 million acres under irrigation through a 2,800-mile network of canals and tributaries when it is completed in 1965. Its two dams will also help to bring under control the destructive Sutlej, longest river in the Punjab. In West Bengal the Damodar Valley Project is intended to bring another one million acres under irrigation. In the eastern state of Orissa, one of the world's mightiest earth dams will irrigate two million acres. In the north a dam will control the Kosi, the "river of sorrows" which annually plunges down from the Himalayas to ravage vast areas, and will supply the Indian state of Bihar and neighboring Nepal with water for 1.6 million acres. Together, the completed river projects, those still under construction and those planned eventually will irrigate a total of some 90 million acres, some 10 per cent of India's total land area (see map, page 104).

The river valley projects are at the core of India's governmental industrialization program, which is also (for the present at least) taking place largely outside the cities. As of 1961 the projects were producing 19.8 billion kilowatt-hours of power per year. This is a substantial increase over 1951, but still not enough for the existing demands of Indian industry.

As yet, Indian manufacturing output is minuscule. In fact, some of the products that Indians like to talk about are not completely Indian. The country produced 22,029 cars in the 1960-1961 production year. Included in that total were 11,351 "Hindusthans," small vehicles based on English designs. Until a few years ago, almost all of the Hindusthan's parts, including even the "Hindusthan" name plate, were manufactured not in the company's Calcutta plant, but in England for assemblage in India. The company has made enormous production strides. But even today, some 25 per cent of the car's parts are imported. More important to a land in which admittedly few people can buy autos, however, is the fact that each year India manufactures a million of the bicycles which fill the cities' streets. In 1960, the bicycle manufacturers were even able to begin a modest overseas trade, and exported 10,000 to the Middle East.

YET India has enormous capacities for industrial growth. "It is one of the few underdeveloped nations in the world," commented U.S. Ambassador John Kenneth Galbraith in 1961, "which is capable of absorbing large amounts of capital, and heading for take-off development." In northeastern India, in the state of Bihar, lie some of the largest deposits of high-grade iron ore in the world, and these are fortunately located close both to good coal deposits and to the port of Calcutta. It was just such an arrangement which, in conjunction with a fund of technical skills, made the German Ruhr the industrial heartland of Europe during the last century, and both Indians and foreign investors are well aware of the comparison. "The state of Bihar," remarks a pamphlet published by the First National City Bank of New York, ". . . could, in time, become the Ruhr of Asia."

While India is still far from having its own

Ruhr, the nation is indeed making indisputable strides toward industrialization, a development which may someday transform city, town and country. In 1960 the nation produced 3,300,000 tons of steel, a rise of 600,000 tons over the 1959 output, and it exported some 150,000 tons of pig iron and steel. India also supplies some 75 per cent of the world's mica and is one of the largest producers of manganese. Since 1948 the country has also increased its production of coal from 30 million tons a year to 50 million, more than quadrupled production of aluminum from 3,400 to 16,000 tons a year and increased output of chemical fertilizers by 180 per cent.

Few of these accomplishments, it must be said, could have been achieved without aid from other nations. Since independence was gained in 1947, India has received more than four billion dollars in loans and grants from foreign sources; a total of some $3.8 billion came from the United States and some $800 million from the Soviet Union. The Soviet Union built the steel mill at Bhilai in central India; the British, the Durgapur plant in West Bengal; and West Germany, a mill in Rourkela.

Moreover, not all of India's planners are convinced that the concentrated effort to establish heavy industry—and the funneling of the country's limited funds in that direction —is appropriate for the economy. "In an [agricultural economy] it is essential that desperately scarce capital should find its way to the small farmer and factory proprietor," remarked the economist B. R. Shenoy in 1960. "Central planning, plus big government spending, must . . . be held responsible for what is perhaps the most troubling aspect of the Indian economy —namely, inflation."

DESPITE such criticism, however, India has set itself on the road to a planned industrialization. "We have seen the successes that have come out planning. . . ." Nehru wrote recently. "We are engaged in a tremendous co-operative adventure. . . . If we want India to go ahead we must industrialize and not

concern ourselves with little factories. . . ."

Such matters are of intense concern to the citizens of India's cities. At present the urban people are not especially affected by the economic changes in the outlying regions. The great dams, the power stations and the factories being established in the hinterlands will inevitably have a more immediate effect upon the people of the villages. It is they who will benefit from the irrigation, who will receive electricity for the first time and who will supply the labor for the new industries. But the city people are aware that their lives also will, in time, be altered by the vast developments afoot in their ancient land. The prospects of change are discussed often—at the endless cocktail parties at which diplomats, bureaucrats, and sari-clad beauties mingle in gossipy, governmental New Delhi, the capital; in the teashops and offices of businesslike Calcutta; and in the shipping headquarters, film studios, publishing houses and advertising offices of the cosmopolitan port of Bombay.

INDIVIDUAL as the Indian cities are in personality, almost all of them share one economic characteristic: shopkeeping is everywhere a major occupation. A merchant may be a man who presides over nothing more than a small square of cloth on which he has placed a few spices; or he may boast a colorful shop cluttered with multihued saris, rich brocades and ivory carvings. As in the rest of Asia, the most popular shopping centers are the infinitely colorful bazaars, but there are also polite establishments where solicitous clerks escort customers to the door and small boys carry packages swiftly to the patrons' waiting cars.

Many of the Indian cities were transformed in varying ways by the streams of refugees who poured into them after the India-Pakistan partition. The problem of the refugees was all the more complex because the Moslems who migrated from the cities to Pakistan were mostly laborers, mechanics and artisans, while the incoming Hindus were businessmen, shopkeepers and clerical workers. The newly arrived

Hindus could not find employment in their own crowded vocations, while the jobs abandoned by the Moslems went unfilled. Delhi alone was inundated by half a million refugees.

Some of these fortuneless people were resettled in homes left by the city dwellers who had emigrated to Pakistan, while others ended up in suburban refugee centers. But, despite intensive efforts, it will be several years before sufficient new housing is available to absorb them all. Many refugee merchants threw together small shacks and went into business immediately. In the years since then many of these small and rickety establishments, spruced up, painted and reinforced, have become highly popular and successful retailing centers.

The vast majority of city dwellers come from the villages, or are only a generation or two removed from them. A great many young men who immigrate to the cities to find jobs leave their wives and children back home with the joint family until they are in a position to establish a home. This process often takes years, but the separation of families is so common that the custom is taken for granted.

Among the jobs most eagerly sought are those in the central government's Indian Administrative Service. One of the lingering effects of British rule is the fact that government service even today carries enormous prestige in India, and a young man who passes the competitive examinations for the I.A.S. can demand a dowry of $4,000 to $10,000 from the father of his prospective bride. Doctors and engineering graduates command about the same amount, but a mere college graduate may get only $2,000. A plain solid citizen is likely to receive only $1,000.

THE reason dowries come into the matter of career choice is that all but an extremely small number of marriages are still arranged in India. Although the country's educated classes may be in revolt against some things, they have not yet seriously challenged the institution of bride choosing. Legislation to outlaw dowries has been enacted, but it is doubtful that the law will be heeded at first. In time, of course, it might be accepted like most other innovations in India.

In New Delhi, the expansive city which the British constructed as their capital on the ruins of seven former imperial cities and which became India's own capital in 1931, the typical city dweller is a modest government employee like Kishan Grover. At 31, Grover is a linotypist who earns about $60 a month from the Government of India Press, and he lives with his family of four in two tiny rooms on the ground floor of one of the boxlike, identical government housing colonies which have been built by the public works department. Grover and his 26-year-old wife, Pushpa, are almost pathetically grateful for their accommodations, for New Delhi's housing shortage remains acute. The rent, which is deducted from Grover's government paycheck, comes to only six dollars a month, and since the apartment is on the ground floor the family have access to a small yard where they can sit in the torrid evenings of the long New Delhi summer.

BEFORE they obtained the apartment, the five Grovers lived in a single room in another section of New Delhi and had to pay nine dollars a month. The family's situation is much better now, but Grover is gloomily aware, as is every other government worker, that his rigid income is not elastic enough to cope with the rising prices of food in New Delhi. With the savings he has accrued, Grover has even managed to make a $126 down payment on a tiny plot of land across the river from New Delhi in suburban Shadra, and someday he hopes to build a house there. He has $105 to go to pay off the balance of the purchase price. To maintain his monthly payments of $21, he has had to make some sacrifices. "It means that my family and I have to deprive ourselves of some things," he says. "We have stopped going to movies, and I no longer go to the coffeehouse with my friends."

After the family moves, moreover, Grover's commuting problems will be increased. New

Delhi is the fastest-growing large city in India (its population has climbed from 1.4 to 2.3 million since 1951, an increase of 63 per cent), and its expansion has far outstripped the capacities of its public utilities. Distances are great, taxis expensive and buses slow and few and far between. As it is now, Grover bicycles a distance of 14 miles a day to and from work, and he will have farther to go when and if he moves to the new place in Shadra. But he thinks the investment will be worth it. When the house is built—as a government employee he can obtain a federal housing loan to begin its construction—he will be able to rent out some of his space for $21 a month. He will also save the rent on his old apartment. The bright future of India, Grover hopes, is "only a few years away."

In crowded Calcutta—the city which the British used to try out new educational methods—similar financial problems plague Professor Durgasaran Chakraborti, who is 53. He has been teaching Sanskrit at Vidyasagar College for 26 years. When he started as a young instructor, he earned $21 a month. Today, as head of the Sanskrit Department, he draws $105 a month, and in wealthy, booming Calcutta, center of a 10-million-ton shipping industry and a number of successful light industries, rents are as high as in New Delhi. Professor Chakraborti and his wife and six children live in four small rooms in a dingy house in Calcutta which, like all the others near it, has not been whitewashed for decades. The location's sole advantage is that it is only a quarter of a mile away from the college and Professor Chakraborti is able to save bus and tram fares by walking to work. The rooms are so cramped that he is ashamed to invite any but his most intimate friends there.

One of Professor Chakraborti's primary domestic concerns is that, lacking dowry money, he has been unable to get his 23-year-old daughter married. He is worried, too, about his eldest son, 21-year-old Dilip, who holds a science degree but has been unable to find employment in an India whose industry cannot at present absorb all of the available graduates. Despite his pride in his son, Professor Chakraborti deplores the over-all trend toward technological studies. "The students today are crazy about science," he says, "but they should remember that India was famous for its philosophers, poets, writers and musicians." He becomes very angry when he thinks about how the Communist party keeps an eye on the more brilliant of the students at the universities and sometimes lures them into the party, and he is annoyed that some of his colleagues have been drawn into the vortex of Indian politics. "Good scholars," he says, "have little time for the game of politics." Professor Chakraborti describes his life and career as "a grind of sacrifice with no financial benefits to show for it."

For all his concern over India's future and his own economic worries, he remains cheerful and unsoured, because Calcutta is a city that affords many intellectual rewards. It has good libraries and reading rooms and a host of eminent thinkers. "There is always pleasure in holding discussions with good scholars," says Professor Chakraborti.

If Calcutta is vigorous, Bombay is India's most disciplined city. Like most big Indian centers it has had its share of bloody riots,

THE EVOLUTION OF A CAPITAL

The capital of India is New Delhi, an administrative center begun in 1911 by the British. On the plains five miles to the north of it is the old city of Delhi, which was once the capital of the Mogul Empire. Although Indians occasionally refer to New Delhi as "Delhi," the two are quite distinct. When the British built the new city they were following an old imperial tradition. Since the 13th Century, when Turkish invaders established Delhi as the home of their sultanate, successive Moslem dynasties each had erected a new edition of the imperial city adjacent to the palaces and fortresses of the old one. The city known today as New Delhi is actually the eighth version of the city.

but it is one of the few whose citizens invariably abide by traffic regulations. Even when no policeman is in sight, drivers refrain from honking their horns in silence zones. In other cities, a policeman's life is likely to be in jeopardy if he interferes with a pedestrian's liberty to walk across the street at will; not so in Bombay, which is the only place in India where jaywalking is actually punished. It is also the only city where passengers docilely line up at bus stops, and where they do not jump onto moving buses.

SUCH orderliness does not mean that Bombay is dull. Lying on the main sea route connecting Europe with the Far East, it has for centuries been enlivened by the constant arrival of foreign visitors. It is India's wealthiest city. The Indian textile industry was flourishing there as early as the 1860s. New industries such as plastics manufacturing gravitate toward it. When India began experimenting with nuclear power, the decision was made almost automatically to set up the country's first atomic reactor in Bombay.

Much of Bombay's liveliness is attributable to its prominent citizens, the Parsis. Descended from Persian fire worshipers who migrated to India in the late Eighth Century, many Parsis had and still have an apparently innate commercial talent coupled with great adaptability. One sign of this in the past was their willingness to shed their given names and adopt the trade names of their professions. This has resulted in their having the quaintest nomenclature of any group in India. Parsis named Doctor or Engineer are common as are such names as Screwallah (a man who deals with screws or hardware) and Bottlewallah (one who deals with bottles). Many Parsis have gone into banking; it is almost impossible to cash a check in Bombay on a Parsi holiday. They were the first Indians to move into apartments, and they play a role in business and government far out of proportion to their numbers. The Tatas of Bombay, India's great industrial family, owners of the iron- and steel-works at Jamshedpur,

largest integrated steel plant in the British Commonwealth, are of Parsi origin.

Typical of Bombay workers is Yeshwant Balla Waiangaonkar, a 38-year-old spinner in one of the cotton mills which help to make Bombay a major center of the Indian textile industry. A villager who came to Bombay 17 years ago from his native region of Maharashtra, Waiangaonkar is a skilled worker squeezed between the rising cost of living and the periodic layoffs caused by the increasing automation of his industry. Married at 16, he now has five children and lives in a thatched hut in one of Bombay's slum districts. When work is available, he earns about one dollar a day, and his monthly income averages about $18. "What can a man with five children hope to do with this amount?" he asks.

WAIANGAONKAR'S special pride is Shantaram, his 16-year-old, eldest son. Shantaram until recently was a top-ranking student who had won several small scholarships. His education, however, was obtained in the Marathi language common in the Bombay area, and he has never learned English, a prerequisite to advancement in many fields.

"He wanted to go ahead and learn English," says his father, "and I managed to spend 12 or 13 rupees [about $2.60] in school fees for him to learn it. But he realized how hard this was for me, and when a job was offered him at 40 rupees a month he took it. He thought he could work by day and study English at night, but by the time he gets home from work it is almost 9 p.m., and he is too tired." Shantaram himself has accepted his fate philosophically. "When our stomachs are not full," he says, "how can I continue to have fond dreams of learning English?"

Waiangaonkar is unhappy, too, about his two-year-old daughter, Vasanti. She has only one dress, and Waiangaonkar wonders whether she does not yearn for new and colorful ones. "I hope for my children's sake," he says, "that things will improve in India." It is a hope devoutly shared by all of India's planners.

As the noise of the city wells up from below, a woman peers out of the shuttered window of an apartment dwelling in Bombay.

Crossroads of the Old and the New

India's cities have long been ports of entry for modern ideas. But many of the urban peoples are former villagers who, while adopting some western ways, resolutely stick to the traditional village attitudes. Meanwhile those who move between the villages and the cities are couriers of the old ways into a new world and vice versa. Usually one side of a city is a stronghold of modernization, while the other, almost as if cut off by a border, is an outpost of antiquity.

121

URBAN BAZAAR in Jaipur engrosses marketers such as these examining a display of pottery. Fabrics and food are also sold. Prices are endlessly haggled over, a seller asking for more than he expects, a buyer offering less than he is willing to pay.

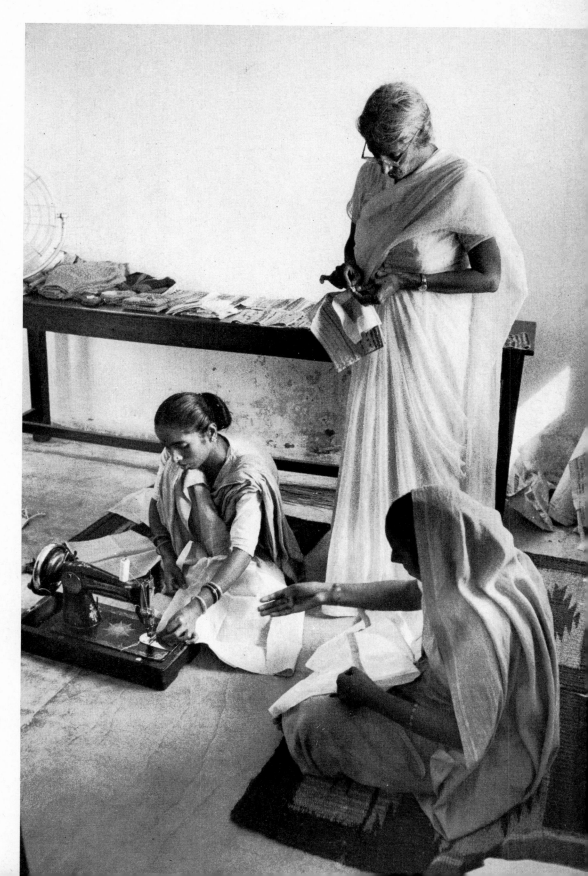

HAND PRINTING of fabrics goes on in cities like Ahmedabad, where a girl in a street stall (*opposite*) assiduously applies an intricate pattern to a cutting of cloth.

MACHINE SEWING, introduced in order to further the Indian's inherent ability with thread, engrosses two Lucknow girls as an intent teacher oversees their progress.

LONG WALL of the Tunga-bhadra dam (*opposite*) dwarfs laborers working on its mile-and-a-half expanse. Tunga-bhadra's reservoir provides irrigation for 830,000 acres.

PROUD ENGINEER points to a sector of the Bhakra-Nangal Project. The world's tallest dam, Bhakra will—with nearby structures—water about 10 million acres.

INTENT FATHER reads on an urban rooftop as his wife gently combs their daughter's hair and a baby naps in the sun. Most of India's educated people live in the cities.

STUDIOUS YOUTHS fill a reading room in the Calcutta National Library, India's main archives (*opposite*). The five-year plans call for extensive library development.

Sitting cross-legged, a dancer gestures symbolically as musicians play traditional instruments. Indian music, puzzling to foreigners,

is purely melodic and makes no use of the principle of harmony.

A Sense of Form and Color

IN few countries is a sense of form and color more closely woven into the pattern of life than in India. Mud walls of villages throughout the land are alive with frescoes of gods, demons, men and animals, executed in yellows, ochers and umbers; those of even the lowliest are ornamented with geometric patterns etched into the drying mud by the artful fingers of a people alive to beauty.

Clustered about the village wells are the women of India, their saris and skirts ablaze with the colors of the empyrean—bright violets, lime greens and vibrant fuchsias. Hems sparkle with gold and silver threads. About their ankles and wrists, metal bracelets jangle in counterpoint to the brass bells hung on the bullocks who tread in nearby fields.

Although pattern and color are integral parts of Indian life, the new India, overwhelmed by problems of politics and poverty, has little time or surplus wealth for the fine arts that once flourished within its borders. In the West, art has been viewed since the end of medieval times as highly personal, an expression of the artist's individual vision of reality. Although there is some artistic activity, notably painting, in the larger cities, India as a whole has little interest in such vanity, even if the country were able to afford to indulge in it. " 'Art' in India and 'art' in the modern world mean two very different things," the late Ananda K. Coomaraswamy, the country's most discerning critic, wrote in 1923. "In India, [art] is the statement of a racial experience, and serves the purposes of life, like daily bread. . . . The modern [western] world, with its glorification of personality, produces works of genius and works of mediocrity following the peculiarities of individual artists." In short, Indian art is—and always has been—a reflection of the country's consummate and continuing interest in the world of the spirit. Whatever the art—painting, sculpture, music, or dance—the arts, India believes, are only a device to lead man toward his eventual union with God. In pursuit of that ideal, anonymous Indian artists have frequently reached greatness.

The many-limbed, many-headed gods of ancient Indian sculpture sometimes have a strange look to western eyes. At times, even when produced in widely separated periods of history, they seem to share an extraordinary similarity, as if Brahma, the Creator, having once made the mold, had guided the hands of his serving sculptors over the centuries. But the sculptured gods are seldom ugly. Sometimes the gods and their followers are depicted in normal human form, beautifully shaped, superbly designed and colored, serene and often unabashed in their enjoyment of life and sex.

THE Aryans who began conquering India some 4,000 years ago apparently employed neither temples nor images in the worship of their nature gods, though the dark-skinned Dravidians whom they conquered apparently did so. India's primitive sculpture, of bigger-than-life kings and animals, appears to represent simple physical energy. Early Hindus also rejected graven images. Bent on discovering the true Self, which they called *Atman*, and convinced that the world is not what it seems and that the Supreme Reality is an invisible spirit, they were swept by a puritanical aversion to worldly arts. Buddhism, when it arose in the Sixth Century B.C., was no kinder to artists, and its monks early forbade the making of images of the Buddha.

IN the First Century A.D., a craving for images arose. Four-armed deities appeared in Hindu temples everywhere in the land. And Buddhism, reversing its ground, emerged as a dominant influence on the art of India. Buddhists carved images first of Buddha himself, then of other Buddhas and *bodhisattvas* (potential Buddhas). The favorite in the Hindu pantheon was Krishna, followed by Vishnu and Shiva in their many guises.

Indian art reached its peak during the Gupta period, from the Fourth through the Sixth Century A.D., which is regarded as the Golden Age of India. High intellectual and spiritual development brought a widespread conviction that all forms and experiences of finite life are reflections of the infinite, and should be freely represented. Power, wealth, and the "utmost sensuousness of experience and expression" combined to produce hundreds of magnificently decorated Hindu and Buddhist temples. Sculpture also flourished. Few of the works executed in the north remain, but many ancient examples, particularly the lively bronze statues of dancing Lord Shiva, survive in central and south India, which were largely untouched by Hun and Moslem invasions.

The earliest Indian buildings, which were made of painted and gilded wood, have long since crumbled to dust. Still standing are the massive stone temples the Buddhists began to construct in the First Century B.C., whose design laid the foundations of an architectural style which was to have an extraordinarily wide influence. Variations of it came to be adopted by virtually all of the countries surrounding India, particularly Java and Cambodia. Many of the Indian forms traveled enormous distances—far into Central Asia and China, and perhaps even to Europe. Some scholars believe that the sweeping open porches, spacious galleries, high-arched roofs and artfully decorated doorways characteristic of late Roman architecture are of Indian origin.

Known as "rock-cut" or "monolithic" temples, the early Buddhist buildings required the labor of generations of artisans. Driving into massive outcropping rock, the builders carved out caves, *stupas* and cells so that entire temples and monasteries could be created underground within huge monoliths of stone. Of India's many cave temples and monasteries, those of Karle, near Bombay, and Ajanta, near Aurangabad, are the best known. Karle inspires awe by its sheer size. Walking between two magnificent entrance pillars, each 50 feet high, the visitor enters a main hall which is 124 feet long, 46.5 feet wide and 45 feet high. The entire interior, including columns and pillars, is covered with sculpture carved from the cave's single mass of rock. Ajanta, more famous than Karle, consists of a series of 30 *viharas* (monasteries) and *chaityas* (halls of worship) extending for more than a third of a mile. Walls and ceilings are brilliant with frescoes executed during the Gupta period, as well as renderings from earlier and later schools.

IN time, Hindu architects and artisans adopted the Buddhist construction technique. But instead of burrowing, they chipped away like sculptors at the exteriors of solid mountains of stone and carved out entire temples in one piece. Few endeavors better exemplify Hinduism's well-known indifference to time. Among the most famous examples of this monumental art are the Kailasa temple at Ellora, the Jagganath temple in Puri and the Seven Pagodas at Mahabalipuram, south of Madras. Later, the construction of such hollowed-out temples was abandoned for more conventional methods. The structures best known today in the West, including the Taj Mahal, the Pearl Mosque in Delhi and others, which have been called

"romance in stone" or "jewelry on a colossal scale," were built by the Moslem rulers, who did not begin arriving in India until the 11th Century. Sometimes constructed by imported artisans, their airy pinnacles and minarets reflect Persian, Egyptian, Syrian and North African influences, interwoven with the Indian style, which laid heavy emphasis on symbolism and the ingenious use of mass.

IF the massive architectural style and the sometimes grotesque, many-limbed deities of Indian temples appear odd to western eyes, Indian music sounds even stranger to western ears, and with good reason. Except for the popular or "film" music which Indians have borrowed from the West, classical Indian music is marked by a total absence of harmony, relying solely on melody for its effect.

The heart of classical Indian music is a melodic form known as the *raga*. Some 70,000 *ragas* exist, but very few musicians have mastered all of them. The musician is given some liberty for improvisation as he performs a *raga*, but must not deviate either from the rhythm or from the basic mood and melodic framework. Each *raga* has a personality of its own and is supposed to be performed only at a particular time or season. Each *raga*, in addition, is dominated by one or more of certain emotions: *bhakti* (intense devotional fervor); *karuna* (sadness, pity, pleading); *shringar* (joy, elation, sensuousness); *veer* (valor, dignity). By concentrating on these emotional elements and by returning after occasional improvisation to the basic theme of the *raga*, the musician creates a hypnotic effect by which he can, according to one western interpreter, "lead his audience through the magic of sound to a depth and intensity of feeling undreamt of in other musical systems."

Dancing, like all the arts in India, is a search for the godhead—"not merely an exercise in body postures, but an act of worship involving the whole body." The Indian passion for symbolism has given a precise meaning to every rhythm, movement, posture and gesture. An

A Sense of Form and Color

Indian government pamphlet notes: "*Tala*, a cyclic system of intricate metrical time-measure peculiar to this country, transforms dance into a mathematical abstraction, and *Laya* or rhythm in all its complexities is but the manifestation of the primal rhythmic energy. Together they are the greatest factors of discipline to help the dancer in his attempt to attune himself to the cosmic content of the Universe."

FOR a brief period some 300 years ago, classical dancing underwent a trying time. Many of the *devadasis*, or temple dancers, turned to prostitution. Some forms of religious dancing became so debauched that they were banished from the temples and performed elsewhere by "nautch girls" who, as one authority delicately puts it, "had a reputation based on other qualifications than art." Such incidents were minor, however. Classical dancing again enjoys its ancient place as an honored and difficult art. (Folk dancing has also made a strong comeback since India's independence.)

One of the chief classical forms, *Bharata Natyam*, has 140 distinct and recognizable poses. A good dancer displays an incredible control over his muscles, especially those of the face, neck and hands. If some accepted dances seem a trifle more erotic than spiritual, the reason is not hard to discover. "So much of our religion in India," explains Shanta Rao, one of India's foremost classical dancers, "is based on the loves of the gods."

In a land so concerned with religion it is hardly surprising that priests, the servants of the gods, were India's first teachers, and that future priests were its first students. Originally both teachers and students were Brahmins, and the curriculum was confined to study of the scriptures. But sometime before 500 B.C. the next two castes—Kshatriyas (nobles and warriors) and Vaishyas (merchants and farmers)—were admitted to the study of the mysteries. Gradually, too, other studies—geometry, algebra, astronomy, anatomy—were added to the curriculum. The Buddhist monasteries, specializing in philosophy, logic and medicine, early became centers of learning, open to Hindu and Buddhist alike. All these influences are reflected in Indian education today. But it was not until the 19th Century, when the British established a university system modeled on that of the University of London, that the formal foundations of higher education were laid. This system, however, was primarily intended to develop English-speaking civil servants for the British administration. Since independence, Indian education has had broader objectives.

The constitution of 1950 set a 10-year goal of free, compulsory schooling for all Indians up to age 14. By 1960, more than 40 million youths were attending an elementary school of sorts. And, building on the base left by the British—and a respect for learning ingrained by centuries of priestly and pedagogical tradition—institutions of higher learning have mushroomed. Before World War II, India possessed only 17 universities, with an enrollment of 125,000. Now there are more than 40 universities, 800 colleges and more than a million students. Many of the new colleges, under trying conditions, are producing well-trained and brilliant young graduates. But, overcrowded, understaffed and underequipped, they are in large part hotbeds of what Indians call "student indiscipline."

INDIAN students strike for easier examination questions, riot over disciplinary acts, rough up each other and professors, squabble over campus and national politics and defy police with stones and tear gas. One reason is that the poor and overcrowded universities provide them with little other recreation. Campuses tend to be "dusty," with "damp, dark corridors" and "malodorous lavatories," one contemporary critic has noted. The University of Calcutta, with 100,000 students the world's largest, teaches three shifts a day.

Another source of trouble is difficulty with English, which continues to be the usual language of instruction. Prewar collegians were mostly the sons of successful, English-speaking professional men. Now the sons of poorer, less westernized families are pouring in great numbers into the colleges.

Most observers ascribe the "indiscipline" to two principal causes. One is poor teaching. Notoriously overworked and underpaid (they earn $50 to $250 per month), many teachers drone out mechanical lectures which some students do not even bother to attend. "If a list is made of the most demoralized and apathetic sections of India's educated population," says one critic, "the teachers will lead it effortlessly." An even more serious source of discontent may be student worry over the future. The Indian economy simply cannot absorb its eightfold increase in college graduates. Meanwhile, new thousands of applicants and their anxious parents knock vainly at university doors. Denied admission, they and their relatives create political pressures for the founding of still more universities.

Urban coffeehouses are filled with an estimated half a million idle, disillusioned, bitter young men with college degrees who disdain manual work and are disappointed in their hopes for prestigious jobs. "After all," says a member of the government's University Grants Commission, "we are a very poor country."

INDIAN authors, save for a few who write in English for foreign audiences, are faced with financial problems as intense as those of the colleges graduates. Mass illiteracy necessarily confines most Indians to popular ballads and other oral literature. An Indian author realizes only about $100 from the sales of an average novel. He earns the rest of his living by grinding out short stories and Sunday supplement articles at about $10 each.

Fortunately for writers, but perhaps unfortunately for India, the nation's divisions of caste and language have produced a tremendous outpouring of newspapers and magazines. There are more than 7,650 daily newspapers and periodicals published in a score or more of languages, including the top English-language papers, some of which were founded by Englishmen. Their influence is now increasingly being challenged by the native-language press.

At their best, Indian newspapers are dignified, responsible and comprehensive. At their worst, they show a slander and licentiousness rarely found in the West. The worst offenders are the small papers printed in local languages —the so-called vernacular press.

The diversity of publications and readers makes it almost impossible to assess the influence of the press in India. Yet some observers believe that individual newspapers have more impact than their western counterparts. In outlying districts, it is common to see a cluster of villagers hunkered down and listening intently while an elder reads them the news.

OFTEN baffling, frequently contradictory, immeasurably elusive, the Indian cultural heritage yet offers extraordinary rewards. After a lifelong study of Sanskrit literature, the great Oxford scholar Max Müller declared:

"If I were asked under what sky the human mind . . . has most deeply pondered over the greatest problems of life, and has found solutions of some of them which well deserve the attention even of those who have studied Plato and Kant—I should point to India. And if I were to ask myself from what literature we . . . who have been nurtured almost exclusively on the thoughts of Greeks and Romans, and of one Semitic race, the Jewish, may draw the corrective which is most wanted in order to make our inner life more perfect . . . more universal, in fact more truly human a life, not for this life only, but a transfigured and eternal life—again I should point to India."

The French author Romain Rolland added in 1918: "I do not suggest that Europeans should embrace an Asiatic faith. I would merely invite them to taste the delight of this rhythmic philosophy, this deep, slow breath of thought. From it they would learn those virtues which above all others the soul of Europe (and of America!) needs today: tranquillity, patience, manly hope, unruffled joy [as the *Bhagavad-Gita* says], 'like a lamp in a windless place, that does not flicker.'"

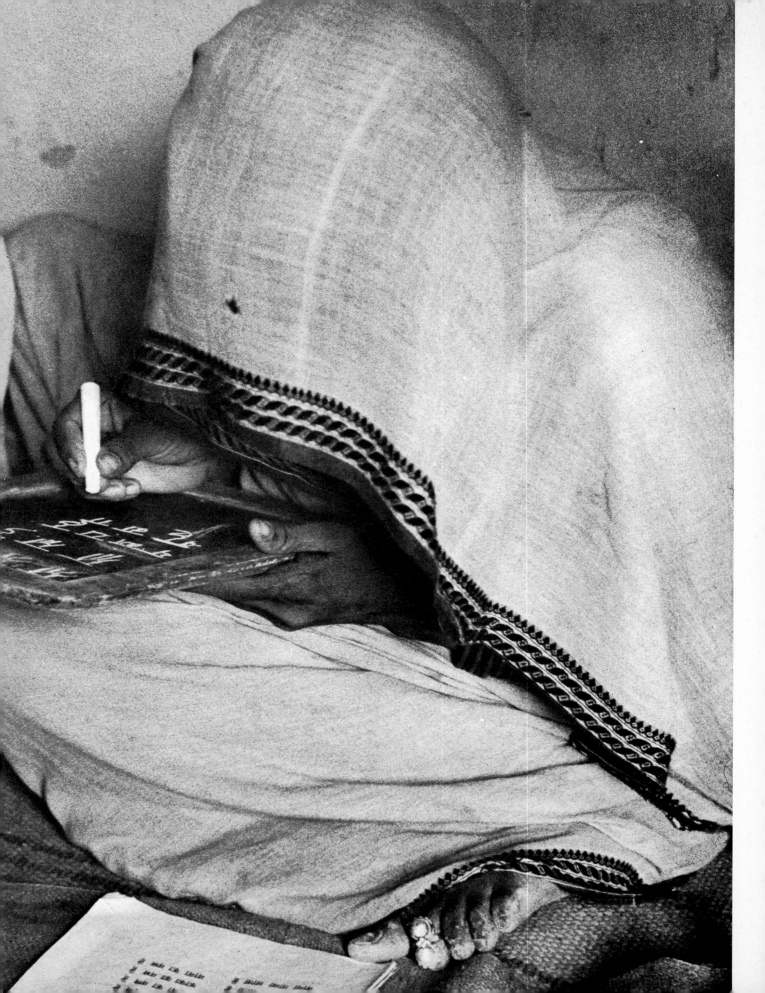

AGED STUDENT, a woman (*opposite*) carefully chalks an exercise on her slate. She is one of thousands of adult Indians now learning to read and write in night classes.

SIDEWALK SCHOLARS study well-worn schoolbooks in a class conducted on a walled street in Jaipur. In many Indian villages, classes meet under a convenient shady tree.

A Varied Culture's Broadening Scope

In India there are some 104 million people who can read and write and some 334 million people who cannot. By law education is free and compulsory for every child between six and 14, but there are still too few schools and teachers. Nevertheless, the expanding government school program and the new village adult-education centers are adding many millions each year to the ranks of the literate. As the dead hand of illiteracy is lifted, India's world of the word —books, magazines and newspapers—quickens with life, sharpening interest in all the new arts.

MOVIE MAKERS *are turning out a few acclaimed masterpieces and hundreds of sentimental melodramas*

FILM CRAFTSMAN, Satyajit Ray (*opposite*) has won world-wide praise for *Pather Panchali*, part of his trilogy of life in Bengal.

COSTUME ROMANCE, a mainstay of Indian movies (*right*), features star actor Bharat Bhushan as a musician in a Mogul court.

DANCE SCENE, another staple attraction, is filmed in Bombay (*below*). India's movie industry is the third largest in the world.

INTRICATE DESIGN of mosaics and alabaster panels decorates a palace built by 17th Century Rajput kings.

JOYOUS SCENE, a painting (*opposite*) depicts Lord Krishna wooing a lady amid the splendors of a Rajput city.

TITAN OF THE ARTS, Rabindranath Tagore is called "the first modern Indian." Philosopher, poet, painter and dramatist, he won the Nobel Prize for Literature in 1913. He died in 1941

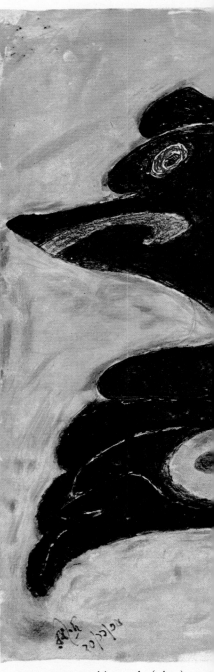

FLOWING FORM, this work (*above*) is one of some 2,000 done by Tagore after he began painting at 70.

BALEFUL LADY, this restrained portrait (*left*) is painted in the primitive, rhythmic style Tagore favored.

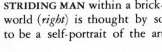

STRIDING MAN within a brick-red world (*right*) is thought by some to be a self-portrait of the artist.

10

Plotting a Lonely Course

ONE question is asked insistently by foreigners who visit New Delhi: After Nehru is gone, who will take over? The subject also troubles thoughtful Indians, but Nehru himself, who is over 70, does not like to talk about it. "I am not a king who picks his successor," he says testily. "When the time comes there will be plenty of good men."

It is not that simple. One of the Congress party's top leaders, Food Minister S. K. Patil, once put the problem bluntly: "Nehru is the greatest asset we have because he is just like a banyan tree under whose shade millions take shelter." But he added that Nehru is also a liability "because in the shade of that banyan tree, biologically, nothing grows."

The Prime Minister may well continue in power for several more years. Yet signs abound that the Congress party, torn by internal quarrels and emptied of the old revolutionary ardor, is very much on the defensive and might be in trouble but for the sheltering branches of the big banyan tree. In forthcoming elections Congress rule will be under stiff challenge in several states, and the party may be forced to govern with a reduced legislative majority.

In the 1957 elections the strongest bid was made by the Communists, who defeated the

145

Congress party in the state of Kerala; but their poor performance in office and, even more, the attacks by Communist China on Indian border outposts have soured many politically conscious Indians on them. This time the challenge may come from elements of the right—Hindu extremists, disenchanted princes trying for a popular comeback, landowning interests alarmed by the government's talk of farm co-operatives—who may succeed in mobilizing big opposition votes in such states as Orissa and Rajasthan.

Congress' basic trouble is that it is no longer a party with a clear mission. Founded to win national independence, it long ago accomplished that purpose and has yet to find another with an equally effective popular and unifying appeal. Factional fights smolder at every level, all basically fueled by bitter differences over caste, religion and local language.

SQUABBLING has even broken out in the top echelons of government, and significantly enough some of the ruckus concerns the question of succession. In the first years of the new nation the forceful Vallabhbhai Patel was at hand as an alternative to Nehru, but Patel died. Unlike Gandhi, who groomed Nehru as his successor, the Prime Minister has failed to train a new group of able young leaders. If Nehru's leadership should end, of course, one of the present members of the Congress party high command might assume leadership. Such a man might be Finance Minister Morarji Desai, an astringent, puritanical administrator. But many Indians expect that when Nehru departs, the Congress party will split up, perhaps along regional or ideological lines.

In that case one possible candidate of any new grouping might be Jayaprakash Narayan, founder-secretary of India's Socialist party, who once spent several years studying at various universities in the United States. He is one of the few Indian leaders with a demonstrated capacity for evoking something of the *darshan* that Nehru establishes with a crowd. Gandhi introduced Narayan to Nehru years ago, and

Nehru once spoke of Narayan as his successor. But Narayan a few years ago became convinced that India's future lies in its villages. Abandoning party politics, he joined Vinoba Bhave, the long-bearded, Gandhi-like ascetic who has persuaded landholders to turn over 4.5 million acres to him for landless peasants. If Narayan should change his mind and return to the political scene with Bhave's blessing, and consequently with the support of the Hindu traditionalists, he might be hard to beat. The possibility of his returning may not be so remote. Narayan took an active role in whipping up public opinion when the Chinese put down the Tibetan revolt in 1959, and he has since continued to speak out against communism.

THE answer, then, to the question of who comes after Nehru is utterly uncertain. This is particularly disquieting because India has become a very important country in world affairs. That India occupies such a place and exerts such influence is in significant part due to Nehru, who has steered the country's foreign policy through the jungle of international politics with considerable skill and daring.

Nehru stated a key aspect of India's foreign policy back in 1948 and has stuck fairly consistently to it since. "We shall take care," he said, "not to align ourselves with one group or another . . . remaining neutral on those [questions] not affecting us directly. . . . India obviously cannot join either of the two blocs." What India would rather seek, said Nehru, was "an understanding between Russia and the United States." In practice Indian diplomacy has divided into three distinct spheres—one dealing with the East-West powers, one with Pakistan and a third with the other Asian countries. India has sought security on its borders, leadership in the efforts of Asian and African countries to influence world affairs and an accommodation between the West and the Communist bloc.

In the world at large, India has aimed at forestalling military conflict between the two major power blocs. This has suited India's own interests because the easing of East-West tensions and the avoiding of military pressures are essential if the country is to raise its appallingly low living standards and industrialize its economy. But this policy also derives from the Indians' deepest traditions. The nation's efforts to act as a bridge between the great powers express values as old as Buddha, which were most recently manifested in the nonviolent methods by which India won its independence.

At international conferences and in the United Nations, India has dwelt on two themes: anticolonialism and nonalignment in the cold war. These themes have won India a following out of all proportion to the nation's military and economic strength. India has taken the lead in mediating between communism and the West—in Korea in 1952, in Indochina in 1956. Attesting to India's place of leadership among the new nations, both the U.S. and Russia have separately sounded out Indian interest in a permanent seat in the United Nations Security Council. (India did not encourage the idea.)

Back home on India's Pakistan borders, however, relations have been conducted on another level. The two nations, born in mutual bloodshed, each regard the other as Public Enemy No. 1, an enmity carrying over from the Hindu-Moslem troubles which caused their original separation. Costly as India's economic programs are, a third of the government's income is still allocated to defense, and its crack troops man the Pakistan borders.

WITH India so active in every international forum, Indian and United States policies have been bound to clash. In the opinion of U.S. leaders, the expansionist threats of the Communist powers could only be contained by uniting all freedom-loving nations in a system of alliances. The Indians have disagreed. "The very process of marshaling the world into two hostile camps," said Nehru, "precipitates the conflict which it is sought to avoid."

Precisely because it has been so tenaciously pursued, Indian policy has been annoying to the United States. And the lofty moralizing in some Indian preachments has been received in the United States with exasperation. To be sure, Indians deeply resented the United States' decision in 1954 to supply arms to Pakistan as part of its alliance-building program. To Nehru this was bringing the cold war to India's door. Indians have feared that Pakistan wants arms not to defend itself against communism, but to strengthen its hand against India.

Although United States-Indian friendship has survived these differences in viewpoint, Americans feel that Nehru has in general tended to be more critical of the West than of the Soviet bloc and that he has used more equivocal terms in discussing Communist misdeeds than western ones. Some Indians try to explain this seeming acceptance of a double standard of judgment by pointing out that one often speaks more openly and frankly to friends than to strangers or enemies. Unfortunately, Nehru has often failed to make this subtle distinction clear to his own countrymen. This has left Indians badly equipped to fend off propaganda from the Communists, as well as that of rightist Hindu groups obsessed with the issue of the U.S.-Pakistan alliance. As a result the average Indian has at times been led to believe that America is his worst enemy.

THE third sphere of Indian diplomacy has been Asia, and it is here that Nehru's policy of getting everybody to abjure the use of force has come to grief. India's aim has been to surround itself with states independent of all outside power—including if possible a Red China independent of Moscow. To that end, India after World War II took the lead in denouncing Dutch "police action" in Indonesia, and called a Pan-Asian conference as early as 1947. Later Nehru evolved his *Pansheel*, or Five Points: "mutual respect for each other's territory, nonaggression, noninterference in each other's internal affairs, equality and mutual benefit, peaceful coexistence." He has signed treaties incorporating this pledge with 16 countries.

But Nehru has constantly had to keep adjusting his position toward China. In 1954, after the new Communist Chinese government had established its supremacy in Tibet and thereby pushed its authority to the very borders of India, Nehru went to Peking and signed a treaty recognizing China's suzerainty in Tibet. Not only did China accept Nehru's *Pansheel* but Mao Tse-tung himself, in Nehru's presence, assured the Dalai Lama (Tibet's God-king) that the Tibetans would enjoy special autonomy.

In the same spirit, India in 1955 arranged to have Communist China invited to the 29-nation Afro-Asian conference at Bandung, and took the lead in the fight to admit Peking to the United Nations. Moscow seemed to approve. The next year Nikita Khrushchev led a whirlwind Soviet good-will mission to India, and large Soviet credits to India followed.

THEN the Chinese began to change their policy toward Tibet. Early in 1959 they shelled the Dalai Lama's residence in Lhasa and mercilessly crushed the full-scale Tibetan uprising that followed. The Dalai Lama fled southward across the Indian border and a great outcry arose in India.

Nehru tried desperately to avoid a clash with Peking (he hopefully reported early news of trouble in Lhasa as "a clash of wills"), and he asserted, "We have no intention of interfering in the internal affairs of China, with whom we have friendly relations." But he soon found himself the target of angry criticism from his own people. Then the Chinese charged that Indians had stirred up the Tibetan rising, and they threw out threatening hints about their "undefined" borders with India.

In the months following, Nehru slowly and reluctantly altered his course. In a dramatic parliamentary scene he uneasily disclosed that for two years the Chinese had been building a road across a corner of India. Now they had also occupied Indian posts along the northeast frontier. As border incidents continued, Nehru warned that any aggression against India's Himalayan protectorates of Bhutan and Sikkim would be considered "an aggression against India." Later he pledged, "If war is thrust upon us we shall fight with all our strength."

Today the Chinese still hold the captured territory—12,000 square miles of it. India has found it takes two to make coexistence, and Nehru's idealistic *Pansheel* policy seems dead. Many Indians have awakened to the menace of Chinese expansionism. One observer has called the 1959 showdown "the most significant event which the new India has come through." Since 1959 there has been a disposition to look on the West with more understanding, and less readiness to take Peking at its word.

The United States has also reassessed some of its policies. In particular, it is not so quick to insist that every country take sides in the cold war. It has overcome its reluctance to contribute large-scale economic aid to a country that acknowledges the same democratic ideals as the West, but insists on avoiding commitment in the cold war. In 1957, when India's second five-year plan fell short for lack of funds, the United States gave India $625 million worth of emergency loans and surplus food. And a symbolic moment in United States-Indian relations came in 1959, when President Eisenhower paid a good-will visit to Delhi and was welcomed by the greatest crowds ever to assemble in India.

ONE of President John F. Kennedy's first legislative goals was to obtain the kind of long-range commitment of foreign aid money that could help India's planning. Aid to India, already approaching a billion dollars a year, may soon become the largest single item in the United States foreign aid program.

Kennedy has said: "No thoughtful citizen can fail to see our stake in the survival of free government in India. . . . Should India fall prey to internal disorder or disillusionment among either its masses or leaders and become absorbed in the Communist system, the free world would suffer an incalculable blow." Beyond question, India and the United States are jointly committed to the difficult experiment of making democracy work in Asia.

Nehru welcomes China's Chou En-lai (left). Next page: Neutrals Sukarno (left), Nehru, Nasser and Tito talk at Belgrade in 1961.

MANEUVERING *carefully between the cold war's bitterly contending forces . . .*

. . . Nehru guides India on an independently neutral course in order to gain precious

time for the painful task of inching the nation toward democracy and prosperity.

Appendix

HISTORICAL DATES

B.C.

c.3500-1500 — Highly advanced civilization flourishes in the Indus Valley

c.2000 — Aryans enter India

c.2000-500 — Composition of the Vedas, the oldest scriptures of Hinduism

c.800-500 — Composition of the *Upanishads*, mystical poetry regarded by all orthodox Hindus as their supreme authority

c.563 — Birth of Gautama Buddha

327-325 — Alexander the Great invades India

c.322 — Chandragupta Maurya founds Maurya Dynasty, India's first northern empire

c.273-232 — Reign of Ashoka, who greatly extends Maurya Empire and establishes Buddhism as state religion. Subsequently Hinduism absorbs elements of Buddhism

c.230 B.C.-225 A.D. — Satavahana or Andhra Dynasty, longest in Indian history, rules over most of central India

A.D.

c.1-300 — Chola, Pandya and Chera Dynasties in south India produce renowned poetic literature in the Tamil language

c.320 — Chandragupta I founds Gupta Empire in northern India

c.320-500 — Golden age of Hindu art, science and Sanskrit literature

c.500 — Gupta Empire disintegrates as Huns and other invaders enter northwestern India

c.550-1200 — The Chalukyas and Rashtrakutas build empires that control the whole of central India

c.600-900 — Pallava and Pandya Dynasties dominate south India

606-647 — Reign of Harsha brings temporary order to northern India

647-1206 — North India disintegrates into a collection of independent kingdoms. Moslems begin invasions from the west

c.900-1250 — The Chola Dynasty unites south India. Art, literature and commerce flourish

1206 — Moslems establish Delhi Sultanate, which reduces nearly all northern Hindu states to vassalage. Later, Moslems invade central and south India

c.1336-1565 — Vijayanagar Empire forms a Hindu bulwark against Moslem incursions in south and central India

1398 — Tamerlane's capture of Delhi ends Delhi Sultanate, leaving the north without a central authority

1498 — Vasco da Gama lands at Calicut

1510 — Portuguese take possession of Goa on the west coast

1526 — Babur invades India and founds north India's Mogul Empire

1556-1605 — Reign of Mogul Emperor Akbar, who enlarges the empire

1613 — British East India Company establishes its first trading station

1628-1658 — Reign of Shah Jahan, builder of the Taj Mahal

1658-1707 — Reign of the despot Aurangzeb, whose costly conquests in central India extend the Mogul Empire but so weaken it that it decays after his death

1707-1815 — European commercial penetration into India

1756 — Nawab of Bengal imprisons English soldiers in the Black Hole of Calcutta; British retaliate with punitive expedition led by Robert Clive

1757 — At battle of Plassey, Clive defeats the nawab, ensuring British domination of Bengal

1772-1885 — British extend their rule over most of India

1784 — India Act leaves British East India Company's commercial affairs relatively undisturbed but subjects its political activities to control by state

1817 — British finally crush power of the Marathas in central India

1824-1826 — British troops conquer Assam, Arakan and Tenasserim

1828-1835 — Under Governor General Lord William Cavendish Bentinck, British establish control over ancient Rajput houses

1842-1844 — Conquest of Sind by the British

1845-1849 — Conquest of the Punjab by the British

1857 — The Sepoy Mutiny or the Great Revolt

1858 — Parliament transfers East India Company's authority to the British crown

1861 — Indian councilors are appointed to advise viceroy and provincial governors, first step toward self-government in India

1877 — Queen Victoria crowned Empress of India

1885 — Organization of Indian National Congress

1885-1947 — Rise of Indian nationalism and the independence movement

1905 — Partition of Bengal into two administrative provinces exasperates Indians and causes acts of violence

1909 — Morley-Minto reforms (Indian Councils Act) greatly increase elective element in provincial legislative councils

1914-1918 — World War I. Indian leaders support the British, who promise to grant greater measure of self-government

1919 — Government of India Act grants reforms which are considered inadequate by Indian nationalists. Mohandas K. Gandhi, leader of Indian National Congress, organizes first of many passive resistance campaigns

1922 — Gandhi and other leaders of the nationalist movement are imprisoned

1922-1929 — Differences between Hindus and Moslems develop in nationalist movement

1929-1935 — Parliament passes the India Act of 1935, which grants a new constitution and sets up elective provincial legislatures

1937 — In first elections Congress party, led by Jawaharlal Nehru, wins majorities in seven of the 11 provinces

1939 — Congress party orders all Congress ministries out of office in protest against British refusal to set a time for independence

1940 — Moslem League under Mohammed Ali Jinnah adopts resolution demanding creation of separate Moslem state

1942 — Britain offers India an interim government during war and full dominion status after war. Congress party demands independence at once and initiates program of civil disobedience. Leaders jailed. Militant elements launch violent "Quit India" movement. Moslem League supports war, gains strength

1946 — British Cabinet mission unsuccessfully attempts to compromise differences between Moslems and Hindus

1947 — Indian Independence Act passed. Country partitioned into two independent dominions. Nehru becomes prime minister of India, Jinnah governor general of Pakistan

1948 — Gandhi assassinated

1949 — India joins the British Commonwealth

1950 — India formally proclaims itself a sovereign republic

FOR FURTHER READING

CHAPTER 1: THE LAND AND THE PEOPLE

Brown, W. Norman, ed., *India, Pakistan, Ceylon.* Cornell University Press, 1951.
Durant, Will, *The Story of Civilization (Our Oriental Heritage, Vol. I).* Simon and Schuster, 1954.
Forster, E. M., *Passage to India.* Harcourt, Brace, 1949.
Garratt, G. T., ed., *The Legacy of India.* Oxford University Press, 1945.
Kipling, Rudyard, *Tales of India.* Rand McNally, 1954.
Lamb, Beatrice Pitney, *Introduction to India.* American Association of University Women Educational Foundation, 1960.
Nehru, Jawaharlal, *The Discovery of India.* John Day, 1946.
Publications Division, Ministry of Information and Broadcasting, Government of India, *Facts about India.* 1953.

CHAPTER 2: HOLY INDIA

Carstairs, G. Morris, *The Twice-Born.* Indiana University Press, 1958.
Coomaraswamy, Ananda, *Buddha and the Gospel of Buddhism.* G. P. Putnam's Sons, 1916.
Eliade, Mircea, *Yoga, Immortality and Freedom.* Pantheon Books, 1958.
The Gospel of Ramakrishna. Beacon Press, 1947.
Guénon, René, *Introduction to the Study of the Hindu Doctrines.* Luzac, London, 1945.
The Mahabharata. Janus Press, London, 1956.
Nivedita, Sister, and Ananda Coomaraswamy, *Myths of the Hindus and Buddhists.* George G. Harrap, London, 1913.
Prabhavananda, Swami, and Christopher Isherwood, *The Song of God, Bhagavad-Gita.* Harper and Brothers, 1951.
Radhakrishnan, S., and Charles A. Moore, *A Source Book in Indian Philosophy.* Princeton University Press, 1957.
Reymond, Lizelle, *My Life with a Brahmin Family.* Rider, London, 1958.
Talks with Sri Ramana Maharshi. T. N. Venkataraman, S. India, 1958.
The World's Great Religions. Time Incorporated, 1957.

CHAPTERS 3 AND 4: HISTORY

Basham, A. L., *The Wonder That Was India.* Macmillan, 1955.
Masani, R. P., *Britain in India.* Oxford University Press, 1960.
Moreland, W. H., and A. C. Chatterjee, *Short History of India.* Longmans, Green, 1957.
Rawlinson, H. G., *India; A Short Cultural History.* Frederick A. Praeger, 1952.

Roberts, P. E., *History of British India.* Oxford University Press, 1958.
Sen, Gertrude Emerson, *The Pageant of India's History.* Longmans, Green, 1948.
Spear, Percival, ed., *The Oxford History of India.* Oxford University Press, 1958.
Wheeler, Sir Mortimer, *Early India and Pakistan.* Frederick A. Praeger, 1959.

CHAPTER 5: GANDHI AND THE REVOLUTION

Bourke-White, Margaret, *Halfway to Freedom.* Simon and Schuster, 1949.
Fischer, Louis, *The Life of Mahatma Gandhi.* Harper and Brothers, 1950.
Gandhi, M. K., *Gandhi's Autobiography.* Public Affairs Press. 1948. *Selected Writings.* Beacon Press, 1951.
Jack, Homer A., ed., *The Gandhi Reader.* Princeton University Press, 1956.
Menon, V. P., *Transfer of Power in India.* Princeton University Press, 1957.
Nanda, B. R., *Mahatma Gandhi.* Beacon Press, 1958.
Sheean, Vincent, *Mahatma Gandhi.* Alfred A. Knopf, 1955.

CHAPTER 6: INDEPENDENCE AND EXPERIMENTS IN DEMOCRACY

Brecher, Michael *Nehru: A Political Biography.* Oxford University Press, 1959.
Griffiths, Percival, *Modern India.* Frederick A. Praeger, 1958.
Joshi, G. N., *The Constitution of India.* St. Martin's Press, 1954.
Moraes, Frank, *India Today.* Macmillan, 1960. *Jawaharlal Nehru.* Macmillan, 1956.
Nehru, Jawaharlal, *Toward Freedom.* John Day, 1941.
Park, Richard L., and Irene Tinker, eds., *Leadership and Political Institutions in India.* Princeton University Press, 1959.
Sheean, Vincent, *Nehru: The Years of Power.* Random House, 1960.
Smith, Donald E., *Nehru and Democracy.* Longmans, Green, 1958.

CHAPTERS 7 AND 8: THE VILLAGES AND THE CITIES

Bauer, P. T., *Indian Economic Policy and Development.* Frederick A. Praeger, 1961.
Chandrasekhar, S., *Population and Planned Parenthood in India.* George Allen & Unwin, London, 1955.
Dube, S.C., *India's Changing Villages.* Cornell University Press, 1956.
Lewis, Oscar, *Village Life in Northern India.* University of Illinois Press, 1958.

Markandaya, Kamala, *Nectar in a Sieve.* John Day, 1955.
Marriott, McKim, ed., *Village India.* University of Chicago Press, 1955.
Planning Commission, Government of India, *The New India.* Macmillan, 1958. *Second Five Year Plan.* 1956.
Rama Rau, Santha, *This Is India.* Harper and Brothers, 1954.
Tennyson, Hallam, *India's Walking Saint; The Story of Vinoba Bhave.* Doubleday, 1955.
Woytinsky, W. S., *India: The Awakening Giant.* Harper and Brothers, 1957.
Zinkin, Taya, *India Changes!* Oxford University Press, 1958.

CHAPTER 9: THE ARTS, EDUCATION AND JOURNALISM

Coomaraswamy, Ananda, *The Bugbear of Literacy.* Dennis Dobson, London, 1949. *Christian and Oriental Philosophy of Art.* Dover Publications, 1956.
Chakravarty, Amiya, ed., *A Tagore Reader.* Macmillan, 1961.
De Bary, William T., Jr., and others, eds., *Sources of Indian Tradition.* Columbia University Press, 1958.
Goetz, Hermann, *India; Five Thousand Years of Indian Art.* McGraw-Hill, 1959.
Mukerjee, Radhakamal, *The Culture and Art of India.* Frederick A. Praeger, 1959.
Rowland, Benjamin, *The Art and Architecture of India.* Penguin, 1953.
Zimmer, Heinrich, *Myths and Symbols in Indian Art and Civilization.* Pantheon, 1946.

CHAPTER 10: THE FUTURE

Bowles, Chester, *Ambassador's Report.* Harper and Brothers, 1954.
Brown, W. Norman, *The United States and India and Pakistan.* Harvard University Press, 1958.
Dean, Vera Micheles, *New Patterns of Democracy in India.* Harvard University Press, 1959.
Harrison, Selig S., *India; The Most Dangerous Decades.* Princeton University Press, 1960.
Nehru, Jawaharlal, *India Today and Tomorrow.* Indian Council for Cultural Relations, Longmans, Green, 1960.
Panikkar, K. M., *Common Sense About India.* Macmillan, 1960.
Seligman, Eustace, *What the United States Can Do About India.* New York University Press, 1956.
Talbot, Phillips, and S. L. Poplai, *India and America; A Study of Their Relations.* Harper and Brothers, 1958.

FAMOUS FIGURES AND WORKS IN INDIAN CULTURE

PAINTING

Satavahana Dynasty (2nd-1st Century B.C.)	Wall paintings in the Buddhist cave temple at Ajanta
Gupta-Vakataka Dynasties (5th-6th Century A.D.)	Paintings representing the lives of the *Bodhisattvas* (potential Buddhas) at Ajanta
Chalukya Dynasty (6th Century)	Paintings in the Viashnava cave at Badami
Pallava Dynasty (7th Century)	Paintings in a cave temple at Sittannavasal; Kailasanatha temple paintings at Kanchipuram; Shiva temple paintings at Panamalai
Chola Dynasty (11th Century)	Brihadisvara temple paintings at Tanjore
Pala Period (11th-12th Century)	Buddhist Mahayana manuscripts on palm leaf, illustrated with paintings of the Buddha and his followers
Western Indian Period (11th-16th Century)	Beginnings of painting on paper, mainly adornment of Jain religious texts: Kalpasutra paintings found at the site of modern Jaunpur, and the Kalpasutras, or aphorisms, painted at Mandu
Sultanate Period (13th-16th Century)	Beginnings of Islamic painting in India: collections like "Jami-al-Tawarikh," a pictorial historical record. Few of these formal sketches are extant
Mogul Period (mid 16th-18th Century)	Miniature paintings in the imperial court of Emperor Akbar depicting Hindu and Persian lore and legend, showing Persian and early western influences. Master painters of Akbar's school, Daswanth and Basawan; flowering of school and portraiture under Emperor Jahangir's patronage
Rajasthani Period (late 16th-19th Century)	Paintings using Hindu themes, particularly the recurring one of the life and amours of Lord Krishna; Ragamala paintings personifying the "Ragas" and "Raginis," or melodic forms, of Indian music
Deccan Period (late 16th-18th Century)	Rich depiction of court life by the Deccan school, influenced by the Persian and Mogul schools; portraiture of nobles; continuation of Rajasthani personification of the "Ragas" and "Raginis"
Pahari Period (late 17th-19th Century)	Sentimental school famous for exquisite linear qualities: mainly devoted to scenes which again describe the loves and life of Krishna. Two of the better known divisions of this Pahari (Hill) school are Basholi (late 17th-mid 18th Century) and Kangra (late 18th-early 19th Century)

SCULPTURE AND ARCHITECTURE

Mauryan Dynasty (3rd Century B.C.)	Didarganji Yakshi, a fragment of a larger sculpture showing an attendant nymph
Sunga Dynasty (2nd Century B.C.)	Bharhut railing, a balustrade of red sandstone with sculptures depicting the Buddha's life. Beginning of India's indigenous school of sculpture
Early Satavahana (2nd-1st Century B.C.)	Eastern and northern gateways of the Sanchi *stupa*, a dome-shaped earthen mound under which relics of the Buddha are believed to be buried
Ikshvaku (2nd Century A.D.)	Rock *stupas* at Nagarajunakonda with panels illustrating the Buddha's birth
Gupta Dynasty (4th-6th Century)	Temple at Deogarh, near Jhansi, famous for its images of Shiva, Vishnu and other Hindu deities. Considered by some authorities a notable example of Indian art
Vakataka Dynasty (4th-6th Century)	Cave sculptures at Ajanta and Ellora: renowned examples of the tendency of Indian art to mix architecture, sculpture and painting
Pallava Dynasty (7th-9th Century)	Beginnings of rock-cut architecture in Tamil area
Western Ganga (9th-10th Century)	Colossal statue at Sravanbelgola of Gomatesvara, the Jain saint
Chola Dynasty (9th-13th Century)	Brihadisvara temple at Tanjore; Airavatesvara temple at Darasuram
Eastern Ganga Dynasty (12th-13th Century)	The Black Pagoda at Konarak, a temple dedicated to the Sun God

Early Pandya Dynasty (7th-8th Century)	Kalugumalai temple cut out of rock
Hoysala Dynasty (12th-13th Century)	Halebid, Belur and Somnathpur temples
Vijayanagar Dynasty (14th-17th Century)	Temples at Hampi, Vellore, Chidambaram, Tiruvannamalai and Kanchipuram
Kakatiya Dynasty (12th-13th Century)	Warangal, Hanamkonda and Palampat temples
Moslem Era (13th-19th Century)	Qutub Minar at Delhi, best example of early Indo-Islamic architecture; Atala Devi Mosque at Jaunpur; tomb of Adil Shah at Bijapur; tomb of Emperor Sher Shah at Sasaram; tomb of Emperor Humayun, earliest example of Mogul architecture, crowned by the broad, rounded dome characteristic of the Indo-Saracenic style later to reach perfection in the Taj Mahal; fort at Agra; Buland Darwaza, a victory gateway at Emperor Akbar's deserted capital, Fatephur Sikri; the Red Fort at Delhi, built by Emperor Shah Jahan; the Jama Masjid in Delhi, the largest mosque in India; the Taj Mahal at Agra, built by Shah Jahan

LITERATURE

Sanskrit (300-150 B.C.)	The *Vedas*—the sacred hymns of Rig, Yajur, Atharva, Sama *Ramayana*, epic by Valmiki *Mahabharata*, epic containing the *Bhagavad-Gita* *Nirukta*, treatise on etymology by Yaksa *Ashtadhyayi*, grammatical aphorisms by Panini *Mahabhashya*, commentary on grammar by Patanjali *Manusmriti*, treatise on law by Manu *Arthasastra*, treatise on political science by Chanakya Kautilya *Natyasastra*, disquisition on the dance and drama by Bharata *Kamasastra*, discourse on love by Vatsyayana *Mrichchhakatika*, drama by Sudraka *Abhijnanasakuntalam*, drama by Kalidasa
Buddhist (3rd Century B.C.-13th Century A.D.)	*Charaka Samhito*, scientific work on medicine *Dhammapada*, quintessence of the Buddha's teachings *Tripitaka*, collection of the Buddha's teachings *Amarakosa*, verse lexicon by Amarasimha *Brihajjataka*, treatise on astrology and *Brihatsamhita*, treatise on astronomy, both by Varahamihira *Harshacharita*, biography of King Harsha by Bana *Isvarakusumanjali*, essay in logic on the existence of God by Udayana *Kathasaritsagara*, volume of stories by Somadeva *Lilavati*, treatise on mathematics by Bhaskara *Rajatarangini*, verse history of Kashmir by Kalhana *Sangitaratnakara*, treatise on music by Sarangadeva
Hindu (14th-17th Century)	*Dohas* and *sakhis*, pithy verses on religion and social mores by Kabir *Sursagar*, collection of verses describing episodes from Krishna's life by Surdas *Ramacharitamanasa*, the story of Rama's life by Tulsidas, poet and teacher
Modern (19th-20th Century)	*Divane Ghalib*, collection of verses in Urdu language by Ghalib, Urdu poet *Gitarahasya*, commentary on the *Bhagavad-Gita* by Bal Gangadhar Tilak *Gitanjali*, collection of poems by Rabindranath Tagore, poet, novelist and artist *Bharatiyar Padalgal*, collection of poems and songs by Subramanya Bharati, a Tamil nationalist poet *Godan*, a novel in Hindi by Premchand, who also wrote in Urdu *Devadas*, tragic novel in Bengali by Saratchandra Chatterji *Bange Dara*, collection of nationalistic poems in Urdu by Muhammad Iqbal *Indian Philosophy* and *Hindu View of Life* by Sarvepalli Radhakrishnan, an English-language interpretation of Indian philosophy *Gitika*, collection of verses by Suryakant Tripathi Nirala, a founder of modern Hindi poetry *Coolie* by Mulk Raj Anand, one of first novelists to write in English *Mr. Sampath*, *The Guide* and *The Financial Expert*, novels by R. K. Narayan *Discovery of India*, letters by Jawaharlal Nehru *The Story of My Experiments with Truth*, by Mohandas Gandhi *Mano Majra*, novel of the 1947 partition by Khushwant Singh *Mary Magdalene*, poem in Malayalam by Vallathol of Kerala *Tyag Patra*, novel in Hindi by Jainendra Kumar

Credits

The sources for the illustrations in this book are shown below. Credits for pictures from left to right are separated by commas, top to bottom by dashes.

Cover—James Burke

8—Marvin Israel

17 through 21—Leo Lionni

22, 23—John G. Ross

24—Leo Lionni

25—Bob Willoughby

26, 27—Margaret Bourke-White, James Burke

28—Henri Cartier-Bresson from Magnum

38, 39—Wallace Kirkland, Margaret Bourke-White

40, 41—James Burke

42, 43—Ellis R. Dungan from Pix

44, 45—Leonard McCombe, Howard Sochurek

46—Marc Riboud from Magnum

47—Dmitri Kessel

48—Vidyavrata from Frances L. Orkin

55, 56, 57—Eliot Elisofon

58, 59—Werner Bischof from Magnum

60, 61—Jack Birns

66—"Christmas in India" by Rudyard Kipling from Rudyard Kipling's Verse, Definitive Edition. Reprinted by permission of Mrs. George Bambridge, The Macmillan Company of Canada and Doubleday and Company Inc.

68, 69—Radio Times Hulton Picture Library—Culver Pictures

70, 71—Marilyn Silverstone from Nancy Palmer Photo Agency—Henri Cartier-Bresson from Magnum

72, 73—Hank Walker

74—United Press International

81—Brian Brake from Magnum

82—United Press International

83, 84, 85—Henri Cartier-Bresson from Magnum

86—T. S. Satyan

93—James Burke

94, 95—T. S. Satyan

96, 97—T. S. Satyan—Marilyn Silverstone from Nancy Palmer Photo Agency, T. S. Satyan, Dominique Berretty

98, 99—Vernon Gibberd

100—Howard Sochurek

104—Map by John M. Woods

108—Eliot Elisofon

109—Howard Sochurek

110, 111—Leo Lionni

112—Ylla from Rapho-Guillumette

113, 114, 115—Henri Cartier-Bresson from Magnum

121 through 124—Leo Lionni

125—Marilyn Silverstone from Nancy Palmer Photo Agency

126—Howard Sochurek

127—James Burke

128—John G. Ross

129—Marilyn Silverstone from Nancy Palmer Photo Agency

130, 131—Henri Cartier-Bresson from Magnum

136—Marilyn Silverstone from Nancy Palmer Photo Agency

137—Henri Cartier-Bresson from Magnum

138—Marilyn Silverstone from Nancy Palmer Photo Agency

139—T. S. Satyan

140—Henri Cartier-Bresson from Magnum

141—Collection of Kumar Sangram Singh

142, 143—Larry Burrows

144—Howard Sochurek

149—T. S. Satyan

150, 151—James Burke

ACKNOWLEDGMENTS

The editors of this book are indebted to the following persons, all of whom read and commented on portions of the text: Paul Sherbert, Executive Director of the Asia Society; Ainslee T. Embree, Assistant Professor of Indian History, Columbia University; and Selig S. Harrison, author of *India: The Most Dangerous Decades*.

Index

This symbol in front of a page number indicates a photograph or painting of subject mentioned.

Text photocomposed on Photon equipment
in the editorial offices of Time Incorporated, New York, New York

•

Printed and bound by R. R. Donnelley & Sons Company
Chicago, Illinois, and Crawfordsville, Indiana

•

Paper by The Mead Corporation, Dayton, Ohio

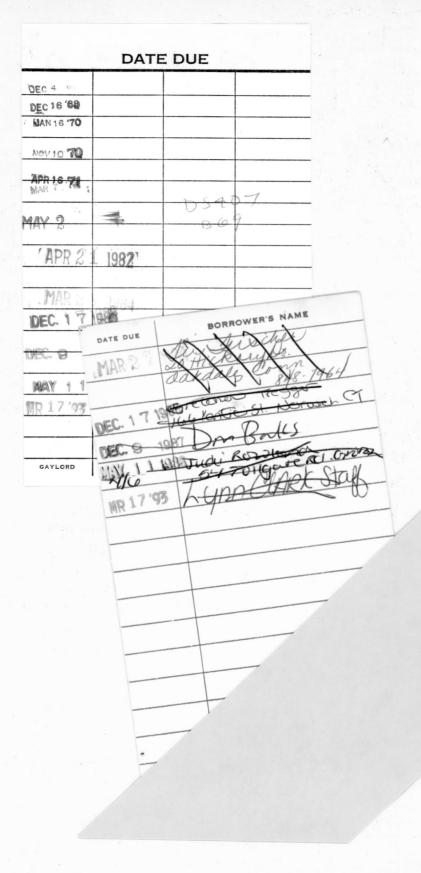

DATE DUE

DATE DUE		
DEC 4		
DEC 16 '69		
JAN 16 '70		
NOV 10 70		
APR 16 71		
MAR		
MAY 2		DS407 B69
APR 21 1982		
MAR		
DEC. 17		
DEC. 9		
MAY 11		
MR 17 '93		

GAYLORD

DATE DUE	BORROWER'S NAME
MAR 2	
DEC. 17	
DEC. 9 1987	Dan Bates
MAY 11	Judi
MR 17 '93	Lynn Clark staff

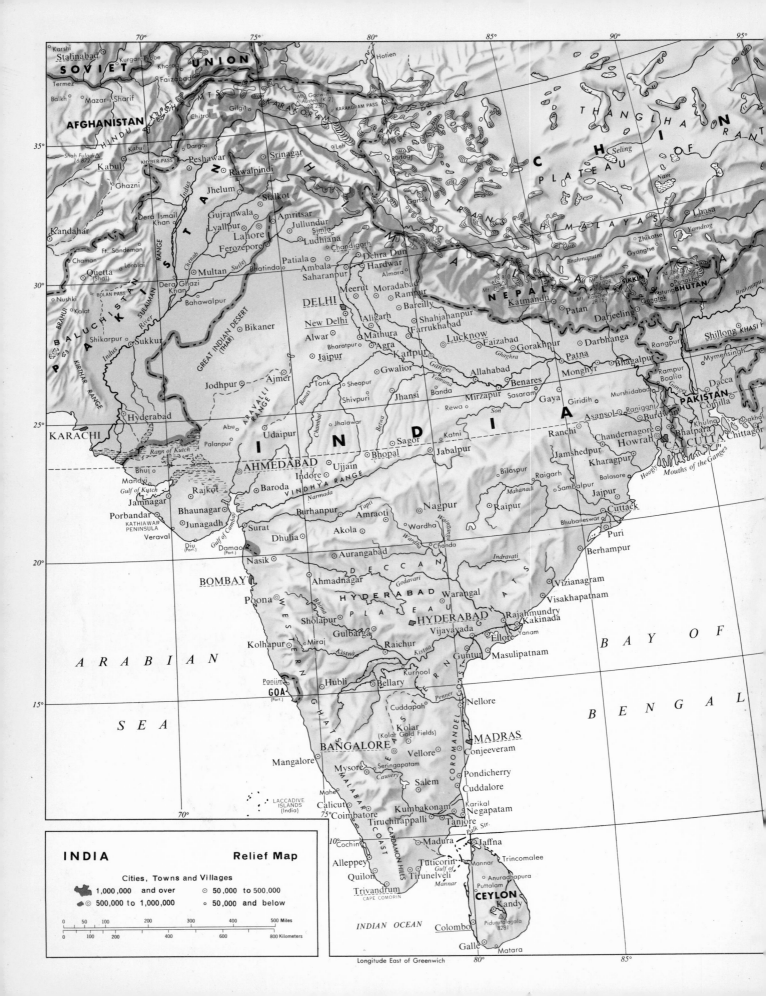

INDIA   Relief Map

Cities, Towns and Villages

1,000,000 and over   ⊚ 50,000 to 500,000
500,000 to 1,000,000   ○ 50,000 and below

0   50 100   200   300   400   500 Miles
0   100   200   400   600   800 Kilometers

Longitude East of Greenwich

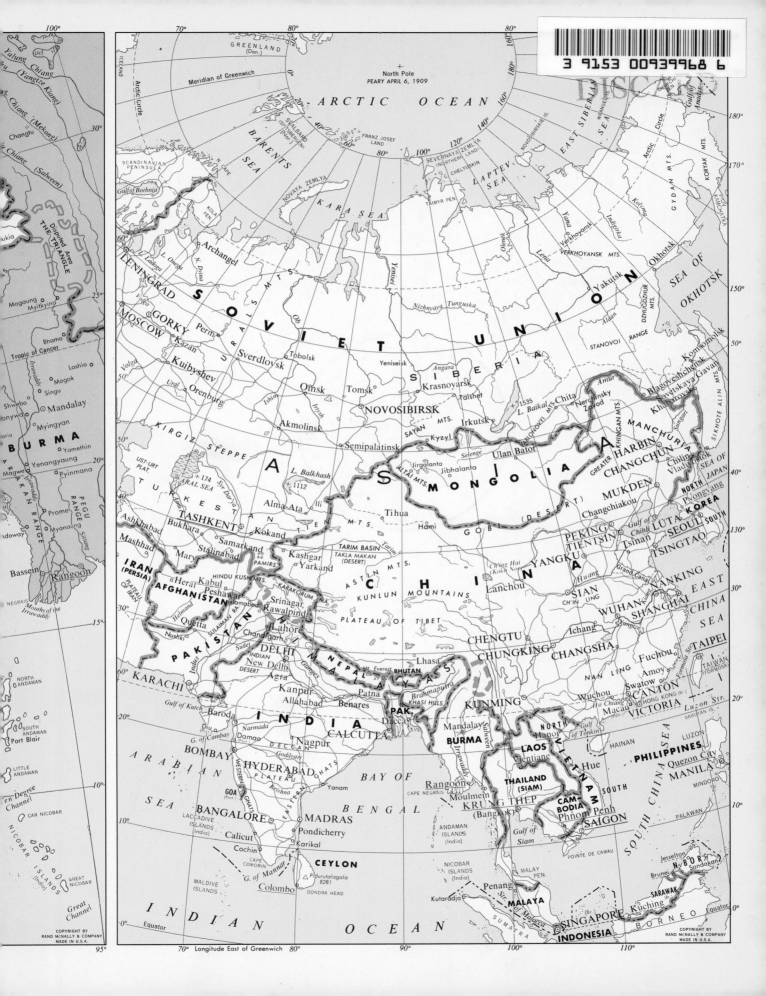